I0081435

DozerDog Domination

DozerDog Domination
The Ultimate Guide to Building an Online Empire

Zack Bordeaux

©2024 All Rights Reserved. No portion of this book may be reproduced, stored in a retrieval system, or transmitted in any form or by any means-electronic, mechanical, photocopy, recording, scanning, or other-except for brief quotations in critical reviews or articles without the prior permission of the author.

Published by Game Changer Publishing

Paperback ISBN: 978-1-963793-50-5
Hardcover ISBN: 978-1-963793-51-2
Digital: ISBN: 978-1-963793-52-9

GC GAME CHANGER PUBLISHING

www.GameChangerPublishing.com

Dedication

To my parents,
who helped inspire me to live the best life possible
and become an entrepreneur.

DozerDog Domination

The Ultimate Guide to Building an Online Empire

Zack Bordeaux

GC GAME CHANGER
PUBLISHING

www.GameChangerPublishing.com

Table of Contents

Introduction

As I lay in bed, attempting to go to sleep, I wondered what I had done wrong. I knew my life's path, but not why I couldn't seem to achieve anything. Just one week earlier, I had been making more money than I ever had in my life—and, although I was only 16 years old, more money than most people I knew had ever made in their lives. I thought I was rich, and I had gotten comfortable.

How could my service have sucked so much that over half of my clients had left me in a week? I have never been fired from a job, but I felt as though I had that night. I felt like a failure and let my feelings get to me. I decided to let my thoughts marinate.

My inner David Goggins kicked in, and I got out of the pout. Then I started a new note on my phone where I wrote down everything I had messed up and how I could correct those mistakes in the future.

What I realized was that the problem was not the fault of my actions but rather my inaction. The epiphany hit me like a bullet. I realized that my service wasn't getting results, and if I wanted to make any money, I was going to have to make some big changes to my business model.

Up until this point, I had run a short-form video agency. There were a lot of problems with this model because the space was getting very saturated and I couldn't provide results that made me any different than the rest of the competition.

So, I started doing research. I joined many online marketing groups and got several mentors. Within a few weeks, I had changed up my entire business model. In this book, I will break down the exact strategies I use to run my business and how I fixed all the flaws of most online service businesses.

One thing I realized as I started to make more money was that I needed to reinvest in my community. The goal of this book is not to make money. In fact, I will probably lose money on it. My goal is to deliver a resource to anybody who is looking to make money online.

I promise you that if you read this book, it will help you leap over the competition and, in just a few days, give you insights that took me decades to learn. If your goal is not to make more money and serve your customers at the highest level, I want you to return this book and not even read it. It will be a waste of time for you. But if you want to level up and make your wildest dreams come true, read this book all the way to the end.

The only way that you can truly reach your goals is by deciding to change your life. *Nothing changes until you change.*

CHAPTER 1

Mindset

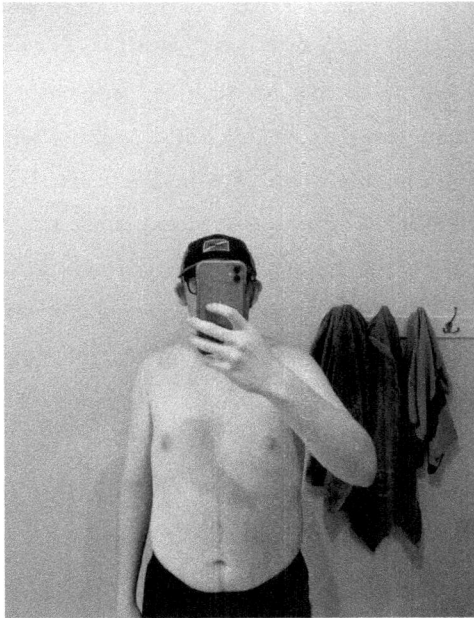

May 19, 2021
11:17 a.m.

    I woke up exhausted after less than four hours of sleep and took my first-ever progress photo. I didn't even have enough confidence to look in the mirror, so I covered my face with my phone. Just one night before, I had lain in bed, scrolling my soul away on TikTok.

After what felt like 10 hours, I scrolled across a video from Riley Jade, a content creator who had done 75Hard, competed in three Ironman Triathlons, and run the Chicago Marathon.

See, Riley and I were the exact opposite. She was fit, and I was fat. She could finish an Ironman, and I couldn't run one mile. She was getting out of the house to run, and I couldn't get out of bed. She was confident, and I was not.

But here's the thing. If I had never seen that video, I would be relaxing six feet under the damp soil right now.

I had no confidence because I had no reason to be confident.

Confidence is a skill, not a trait. Just like the skill of sales, confidence is learned through constant practice. It does not come naturally to me.

I went to a private elementary and middle school with 18 people in my graduating class. Don't get me wrong. I would give everything to go back and live that life for even a day. There was no stress, and I was at ease. I met some of my best friends for life there. But with only 18 in your class, you don't learn how to socialize well. When I went to high school, there were over six hundred people in my graduating class. The biggest lesson this taught me was that the only way to build confidence is by purposely putting yourself in situations that require it.

In high school, I had no choice but to socialize. To this day, I have a very small social circle. If a friend isn't helping me achieve my goals, I can't afford to waste my time on them.

Social Circles

There are two types of social circles: the inner circle and the outer circle. The outer circle is made up of people who are in your life but are not close friends. The inner circle consists of your closest friends. They are typically involved in your personal life and know your deepest concerns. They are the people you can go to in times of need and who will celebrate your wins. To be in this circle, they need to be highly trustworthy and share strong emotional bonds with you.

The inner circle should be small. The more people there are in this circle, the less you will value them. Don't let people into your inner circle if they don't have the characteristics you are looking for, or they will corrupt you and the rest of your circle. This includes people who are part of your life but with whom you don't share a deep bond. They might be acquaintances, colleagues, relatives, or friends with whom you have a more casual relationship.

As an entrepreneur, you have to constantly improve yourself and your business to keep up with the competition. This is a normal process, and it's why I am not a huge fan of the holidays. Relatives will trash-talk you and say, "You have changed."

Yeah. That's the point, dumbass. We should all be constantly evolving. Why would I want to stay the same? Why would I want to be broke my whole life? Why would I want to die because I am obese? Why would I want to "opt-in" to losing?

Change is normal in this game. Embrace it. Pushing past the comfort zone is not always easy for others to understand or appreciate. Some people are built to win; some people are built to be dorks.

When relatives throw shade with comments like "You have changed," remember why that change was necessary in the first place. Staying the same often means staying comfortable.

Comfort is the killer of your dreams.

Almost everyone who comes to me says they struggle with confidence. They are scared of what their family and friends might say. Splitting with your family is a hard choice, but ultimately, they will be the ones asking you for jobs when you have built your empire.

Who cares what they think? Are you really going to let your grandma be the reason you don't dominate life?

Building Your Personal Brand

When I first started building my personal brand on Instagram, I decided to have a page for my business content, a separate page for my fitness content, and a private page for myself and close friends. Do not make the same mistake I did.

Let's talk about my fitness account. I was actually fairly successful in building it up. I built it up to around two thousand followers fairly quickly. What I didn't realize is that followers don't matter; money matters.

When I tried to monetize the fitness account, I realized that since everyone who followed me was already into fitness, they didn't need to purchase my services. I tried multiple strategies to address this, but it was basically impossible.

If you were stranded in the middle of a desert, wouldn't a delicious, thirst-quenching, ice-cold glass of lemonade sound good? Even though it solves the problem, you can't sell lemonade in the desert. Why? Because you can't sell a product if there's no audience for it. It's the same for any business. You need to understand who your target audience is and what they need. That way, you can position yourself as the solution to the problem and make money by doing so.

Starting a new account was a huge waste of time for me, and chances are it will be the same for you. A fitness coach does not target people who are into fitness because those people already know what they are doing. Coaches target people who desire knowledge and a more well-rounded view of the world.

What people want is connection. They want to see a face, and they want to interact with real people. In this world of AI, personal connection is highly valued. Prospects seek authenticity and genuine interactions. Emphasizing human elements in your services, like personalized advice, face-to-face meetings, or even sharing your own experiences and stories, can significantly enhance client satisfaction. People buy from people.

When you show that you are a baller, you inspire the people around you. I look at billionaires on Instagram, and it reminds me that I need to step up my game so I can get to another level. I get it. At first, you don't have anything to flex, but you have to walk around like you are "The Man" every single day.

Normal people will call you ego-driven and crazy.

Normal people are dorks who live in their parents' basement and don't have any money.

To break through, you need to stop caring about others' opinions that are lower than your own. The people who call my content cringe are the same NPCs who play video games and wonder why "the world did them wrong." Don't fall into the trap of entitlement.

I work a minimum of 12 hours a day, not because I have to but because I want to, and at the end of the day, I've given my all and have completely dominated everything that stood in my path.

Success is the pursuit of fulfilling your true potential.

It's your obligation.

If you aren't successful, the people around you will also suffer. Do it for them.

Three Pillars to Personal Success

There are three pillars to personal success: *mindset, muscles, and money.*

Your mindset is the foundation for these pillars. If you remember the story of the three little pigs, the houses of the first two pigs had weak foundations, and they got blown down. The last house, which stood tall, was the one with the right foundation.

The walls of the house represent your muscles. They must be strong and resilient, much like the skills and strategies you apply in your business. Just as the pig who built his house with bricks took the time to lay each one carefully and with purpose, you must take the same approach with your business decisions and strategies. You can't have muscle or money without a good foundation.

Now, here is the thing. You can have a roof (money) without walls, but it is not always going to be stable. While the roof offers protection, it's the walls and foundation—mindset and money—that provide the necessary support.

Adopting a new mindset can lead to gains in both wealth and health. As you build muscle, you often gain the respect of others. Similarly, growing your wealth can enhance the respect you receive.

In personal success, mindset is the sturdy foundation that supports the walls of muscle and the roof of money, ensuring that your structure of success remains unshaken. A robust mindset not only holds your success together but also enhances physical strength and financial stability. With a solid mindset, you're well equipped to develop and leverage your skills effectively.

Skills vs. Traits

Have you ever felt like certain things just weren't in your wheelhouse? For the longest time, I believed that I was simply not cut out for gym life. Maybe some people were born with that zest, but not me.

That was my backstory and the false narrative that I stitched into the fabric of my identity.

The mere thought of working out was synonymous with the discomfort and inevitable sense of failure I had. This wasn't because I lacked strength or stamina. The problem was far more fundamental. I lacked discipline.

This revelation hit me heavier than a dumbbell.

Discipline, contrary to my long-held belief, wasn't a trait that some lucky folks were born with and others, like me, were forever destined to envy.

It was a skill that could be honed, mastered, and developed over time.

Traits are things you're given from birth. Success is a skill, not a trait, just as discipline is a skill, not a trait.

They can be cultivated.

Building Momentum

The knowledge within this book will teach you the skills you need to go out and conquer your life. But without the skill of discipline and the action you must take, you'll never get anything out of it.

Guess what? I don't feel like doing anything on the weekends, either, yet I still get my work done. You have to start embracing difficulty as part of your business journey. You've got to do things when you don't feel like doing them. That's what discipline is, after all.

You can't rely on your feelings all the time. I adopted a strategy that I call the momentum master list. When I wake up, I write down eight to 10 micro-tasks and one master task to do that day. These are things that I must get done before I go to sleep.

As I write them down, I start to plan them into my calendar. Andy Frisella, CEO of 1st Phorm and creator of the 75Hard program, has a similar strategy called the Power List, where you write down five critical tasks that you're going to complete that day and, if you do all of them, you get a win for the day.

The goal here is to build **momentum** because everything revolves around it.

The Business Owners Mindset

When I first went to college at the University of South Carolina, the dining halls were not superb. They lacked healthy options and food I wanted to eat.

At the time, I was on a diet, so I wasn't allowed to eat the cupcakes and crap they were feeding everyone else at the dining hall.

I used to wonder why there was an obesity epidemic in America, and then I went to college. I tried to eat healthy, but it was impossible.

Another thing I learned was that to hit my protein goals, I had to eat eight cheeseburgers a day from the dining hall. Yes, this was the only high-protein option they had that I could eat.

Each time you went up to the grill, you could only get one cheeseburger, and it took around 30 minutes for them to make it. So, for me to hit my protein goal, I would have to stand in line for four hours a day!

I realized quickly that their systems sucked.

Why?

Because they didn't have any.

The system was that you just walked up and told them what you wanted and hoped they made it right.

As an entrepreneur building an empire, you have to constantly look to improve and innovate current business systems out in the world. Next time you go to the store, check out their systems. See how everything works and what you can implement in your own business. There is always a better way of doing things. You just have to find it.

Making Informed Business Decisions

In my second year of high school, I switched to public school from a private school. I made the switch late after registration had opened.

I was the last to be registered for classes, so I didn't really have a huge choice of what to take. One of the classes I was forced to take as an elective was engineering. While, originally, I wasn't excited about this class, I actually learned a lot from it.

Unlike most classes, engineering gave me a systemized view of how to build things as a product. Every time we did anything in engineering class, we wrote out every option we could think of, along with the pros and cons of each.

I still use this framework today. Every time I have to make a hard decision, I write down a list of the pros and cons and think about whether this decision will positively or negatively impact me, my life, and my business: "Do the pros actually outweigh the cons?"

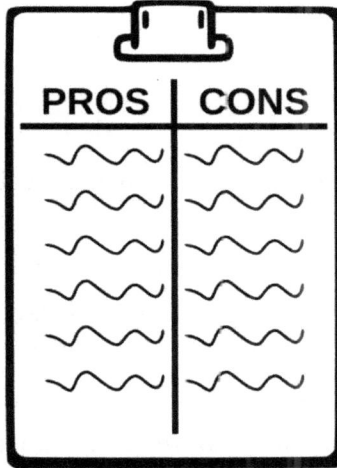

For example, vaping is something that I have never understood. Although there might not be a ton of negative side effects, I don't see any positive effects, either. For me, the pros don't outweigh the cons.

Decision-making is a critical skill in today's fast-paced business environment, and many professionals find themselves stuck in a state of "analysis paralysis." The fear of making the wrong decision leads to a cycle of overthinking and inaction.

Analysis paralysis often originates from deep-seated fears such as the fear of failure or a desire for perfection, which can lead to an endless quest for more information, delaying decisions and stalling progress. When you identify these psychological triggers, you can begin to address and overcome them.

I have made the same mistake many times. I have waited for the perfect time to start something. It could be in my business. It could be with a diet. It could be a number of things. Here is the thing: the perfect time is never fucking coming. Stop waiting for it. Some level of risk is inherent in all decisions we make, and seeking perfection is impractical in a business context.

The repercussions of analysis paralysis extend beyond individual indecision. It seriously impacts the flow of a team, which leads to a loss of productivity. Analysis paralysis also leads to the inability to respond swiftly to market changes.

Overcoming Burnout

This is a real message I got from a digital media manager and podcast host.

"It's come on a day where I'm just not feeling it. Today it just seems easier to hang things up and walk away than to keep struggling through the muck of all of this. I work my day job, then the side hustle (this work), then sleep. Get up the next day and rinse and repeat. I probably just need a time-out, but I have three fresh and new clients who are excited about what I can do for them. I'm just no longer excited."

He felt like many: burned out. I am here to tell you that burnout is a feeling, not a logical thought.

Andy Frisella laid this out well. He says we have two voices in our head: the "boss" voice that builds you into an absolute "G" and the "bitch" voice that tries to hold you back. Frisella says: "The 'boss' voice is the one that pushes you to do great things in life. It encourages you to do shit that takes you closer to your goals. This is the voice that will help you reach your true potential. Your 'bitch' voice operates differently… It's the voice that makes excuses… The voice that fuels self-deflating thoughts… The voice that keeps you from achieving greatness.

When you feed the bitch voice… It will infect every area of your life… FAST." (Source: AndyFrisella.com)

I don't go to the gym every day because I feel like it. I don't feel like driving 40 minutes in traffic to get there and 40 minutes back. But guess what? I do it because I know it is going to improve my quality of life. Same thing with business. Some days, I just don't want to get out of bed. But I do it anyway.

Everyone wants to have a well-established personal brand, tons of money, and a six-pack. **Your goals don't make you unique.** The actions you take to reach those goals are what make you unique. It is not a feeling that gets me out of bed every morning. It is the discipline I have built up over the years.

If I only posted on social media when I felt like it, I would not have any posts. When you lack the discipline to post, you should bring in someone who can do it for you. Results do not come without consistency.

Parallel Leaping

When you reach the big dogs, they will always tell you that you need to move faster. You have to stop overthinking and start thinking more logically.

People often tell me that they want to start a business. When I ask them three months later how their business is going, they still haven't even formed the LLC.

The window of opportunity is real.

So many people have come and gone in this space. That's why it's so important to act with speed.

One thing that sets us apart from most people is the speed with which we act upon our goals. We don't let fear or doubt slow us down. Instead, we take action immediately and leverage the power of momentum to propel us forward.

In most businesses, it should not take a month to go from having a business idea to making money. By the time you're ready to monetize your business, the window of opportunity is already gone.

My goal is to turn decades into days. I want to leapfrog my clients over their competition.

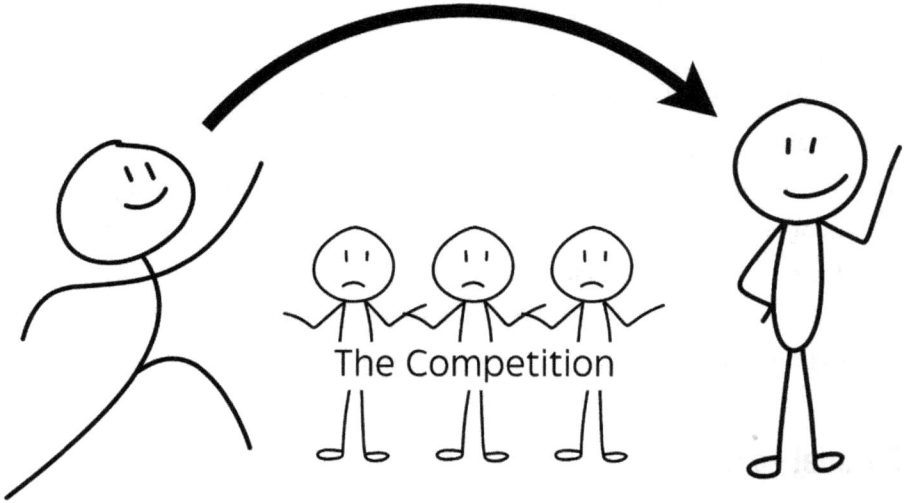

The Competition

The faster you move, the quicker your results will be.

There's a big difference between procrastination and perfectionism. Procrastination is when you put off taking action, while perfectionism is constantly seeking the "perfect" solution before taking any action.

Without execution, an idea is just that, an idea. The fact is, the more you execute, the faster your dreams become a reality.

The Halloween Rule

On October 31, 2011, I implemented a new rule for Halloween: I would limit myself to two pieces of candy per day starting the next morning. Back when I was six, I lacked discipline. I struggled to adhere to diets because I always convinced myself that I would start on Monday. It's a common pattern. We tell ourselves we'll start on Monday, only to postpone it to Tuesday when Monday arrives. In reality, the diet rarely comes to fruition.

I once had a friend who constantly claimed he would have "the greatest comeback of all time." It never materialized. Why? Because he always spoke of doing it in the future.

You see, decisions should be made for the present, not some hypothetical future scenario.

What decisions are you making right now to transform your life?

You must reshape your vocabulary for success. Instead of saying "I should," adopt the mindset of "I must." Replace "I will" with "I am." Erase the words "I can't" and "impossible" from your lexicon; they offer no benefit.

The energy you bring to the table is just as crucial as the words you articulate. I'm not suggesting you act hyperactively; just ensure that the energy you exude is valuable and uplifts others.

Rethinking Goal Setting

I made a video a while back that got a lot of hate. In it, I talked about why I think "SMART goals" are stupid. Everyone talks about setting achievable goals, but I don't believe that is a good strategy at all.

If you achieve your goal, that means you have more to give, and your goal wasn't big enough.

My goal is to make the normies look at me like I'm a dumbass every time I say the size of my goals.

If you aren't familiar with *The 10x Rule* by Grant Cardone, it's one of the most life-changing books I have ever read. Instead of setting my goals at an achievable level, I always set them at 10 times (10x) the size of what I originally planned. This helps me take massive action to achieve those goals.

The top 3% of wealthy individuals have written and specific goals. The top 10% have goals in their heads. The middle 60% have daydreams, and the bottom 20% have neither goals nor dreams.

If your goal is to be in the top 1%, you need to have written and specific goals.

Goal Setting Framework

Here are four unconventional things that I think about when setting goals. The average person will disagree with most of these, and that's okay.

- The average American has less than $1,000 in their bank account.
- The average American is 17 pounds overweight.
- The average American is an NPC who doesn't have any ambitions or goals.
- I do not conform to being average. It's called a standard. Let's raise yours.

The Four Pillars of Goal Setting

If you don't want to be average, you need to set impenetrable goals. Here are the four pillars of goal setting:

1. **Visionary Thinking:** Imagine future possibilities that transcend current limitations, inspiring bold new ideas.
2. **Unrealistic Expectations**: Set goals that stretch beyond the ordinary. Unrealistic expectations push boundaries and ignite innovation.
3. **Massive Action:** Take bold, decisive steps that go beyond your current efforts to achieve your goals.
4. **Persistence:** Relentlessly pursue your goals, overcoming obstacles and setbacks with unwavering dedication.

Make sure you're thinking big and not limiting yourself for any reason. Define your goals in the broadest possible terms. For instance, instead of saying, "I want to start a successful business," you might say, "I want to revolutionize my industry."

While your goals should be specific, they should also be incredibly big. I believe your goal should be so huge that it seems unrealistic. People should look at you like you're stupid every time you say what it is. I have had teachers, family, and friends laugh at me to my face whenever I tell them a goal. They think that I'm joking about it. I'm not. My goals are crazy, but I will achieve them.

Your goals need to push you out of your comfort zone and make you more likely to achieve extraordinary results.

If you're not taking massive action and being pushed out of your comfort zone, you might as well set small goals like all of the average people tell you to do.

Once you've defined a goal, you need to take massive action to achieve it. That means working harder and smarter than anyone else in the space.

You need to be relentless in your pursuit of the goal. This means not giving up for any reason, even when things get tough.

Whenever I'm setting a goal, I always ask myself these four questions:

1. Is this goal making me think and act outside of my comfort zone?
2. Does this goal inspire and excite me?
3. Am I willing to take massive action to achieve this goal?
4. Does this goal align with my long-term vision for my life and my business?

Following Your Passion in Business

In 2017, Campground Accounting was born out of our family's deep love for camping. While my mom had been a CPA since 1992, she realized she needed to narrow her focus. It all started when we began camping in our camper during my childhood. We quickly developed a profound appreciation for the experience and learned firsthand the value of passion in business.

During challenging times, passion serves as a driving force, offering motivation and strength. You don't have to have passion to start a business, but you do need a reason to serve. Consider the example of the person who owns a porta-potty company. Perhaps they aren't particularly passionate about portable toilets, but they are often undeniably successful. Sometimes, it's not solely about passion but also about believing in what you do and leveraging your strengths.

CHAPTER 2

Product and Service Development

As Pepsi became more popular, Coca-Cola faced a big problem. Pepsi was gaining market share with its sweeter formula. The people at Coca-Cola started panicking. *We need to do something*, they thought.

So, they came up with a secret plan. They worked day and night, mixing and tasting, until they made a new drink. It was sweeter than the old one. They called this new drink "New Coke" and were very excited to share it with everyone. "Everyone will love this new taste," they said.

But when people tried New Coke, they were not happy. "Where's our old Coca-Cola?" America asked. Kids missed drinking it on sunny days. Families missed having it at their picnics. Everyone started to miss the old, special taste of Coca-Cola. The people at Coca-Cola didn't expect this at all! They thought everyone wanted something new and sweet, but they were wrong. People wanted their beloved old Coke back.

Coca-Cola learned a very important lesson. Sometimes, what you already have is perfect just the way it is. You don't always need to change to be better. To scale their business, they didn't need anything different; they just needed more of what they already had. Listening to what people really want is super important.

The biggest worry of most businesses is the acquisition of customers. But the richest understand that the amount of customers doesn't matter. It is always easier to sell to people who have bought from you before because they already trust you. If your product is bad, people won't keep buying it.

This is a great example of how good products can affect how a business flows and grows.

The five leading players in service-based industries boast an impressive average customer retention rate of 94% (Source: SurveySparrow). A key factor contributing to this success is the quality of their products. When you've already sold something to a customer, it becomes much easier to sell them additional offerings. For instance, if I've previously sold a video service to someone, it becomes significantly easier to convince them to try our growth marketing service. The rapport, trust, and satisfaction they have with our company and product pave the way for even greater trust in future endeavors.

In my group, the average close rate for upselling new products is an impressive 65%, far surpassing the usual 20%. This statistic specifically applies to customers who have previously made a purchase and are now considering, an upsell.

When you have a great product, it sells itself through word of mouth. This means you don't have to worry about marketing. Some of my most valuable customers and team members have come to me through word-of-mouth recommendations.

In this digital era, everyone has the potential to be an influencer. Anyone can write a review, post on Facebook, or share their thoughts online about a product, good or bad. It's not just good products that have the advantage; bad products also have a way of exposing themselves.

Why is this? Well, it's because everyone easily notices bad products in the market. People rely on word of mouth to determine whether a product is worth considering even before they take a closer look.

In 2005, Dell held a dominant position in the computer market, supplying their products to a wide range of customers. At that time, a man named Jeff purchased a Dell computer with high hopes, only to find it to be of poor quality. He was not thrilled with the purchase and attempted to return it. He reached out to Dell customer support for assistance, but to his dismay, they provided no solution and showed no interest in resolving the issue, essentially dismissing his concerns.

Unbeknownst to Dell, that man was Jeff Jarvis, an influential figure in the blogging world. His negative experience tarnished the company's reputation, resulting in a significant decline in its stock value. The incident, famously known as "Dell Hell," had a lasting impact on the company, leading to substantial financial losses, all caused by the dissatisfaction of just one customer.

This serves as a powerful reminder of the importance of treating every customer as a potential influencer regardless of their following or influence. Wouldn't you treat every customer with utmost care if you knew they had 10 million followers? The truth is, you should treat every customer with equal importance, as you never know who holds the greatest influence or impact.

Product Market Fit (PMF)

Not long ago, an online coach I was working with faced difficulties attracting clients despite her unique holistic coaching approach. It dawned on her that the root of the problem lay in her coaching program, which failed to align with the needs and desires of the market. She tirelessly attempted to sell it but to no avail. Why? Simply because her program neither met their needs nor sparked their interest.

After some coaching, she decided it was time to spice things up. She identified her audience as mid-30s professionals seeking career growth and personal development. Instead of guessing their desires, she engaged with them directly, conducting interviews to understand their needs, aspirations, and fears. Then she revamped her program, focusing on specific issues like work-life balance, self-doubt, and leadership skills.

She did something many coaches don't: she tailored her program to a specific target market and set herself apart from generic offerings. The true turning point lay not only in the program but in how she communicated it through her website and marketing materials. Many people possess unique programs, but they struggle to convey their value effectively.

Now her client base flourishes, accompanied by a wealth of positive testimonials. Her business is thriving, and she is making over six figures every month from her online coaching business.

Product-market fit (PMF) is the art of deeply understanding the needs and desires of customers. It helps you craft a compelling value proposition tailored to specific individuals. This drives business growth through word of mouth and lowers customer acquisition costs (CAC). It also provides a competitive advantage by differentiating a product or service in a crowded market.

PMF helps you avoid the pain of developing a product that doesn't meet the market's needs. Before investing in back-end systems or acquisition strategies, you have to make sure there are people who want your product. This can be achieved by identifying gaps where no existing solution addresses the problems faced by your target audience. Lack of PMF is the number one reason offers fail.

Engaging in conversations with your target audience is the easiest way to achieve this, but data analysis and market research can also help identify potential customers.

Ideal Customer Profile (ICP)

Throughout my years of learning various frameworks, one that has been the most useful is the ICP framework. It addresses a crucial issue I once faced: the lack of understanding about my target audience.

I get it. Niching down is hard, but without a clear picture of the market, I struggled to create and sell products that truly met my clients' needs and desires. It became evident that the first step in developing an ideal customer profile (ICP) is to identify a niche.

Allow me to illustrate this point with an example from my mom's business, Campground Accounting. Her accounting firm specializes in serving family-owned campgrounds across the United States. She has become the industry leader in providing accounting services tailored to the unique needs of campground owners. She found a small group and solved their problems.

There are a lot of ways to find a niche, but my method is called **"the Niche Prism."** This framework entails delving into four key aspects of your target market: their *persona, passions, preferences,* and *principles.*

Persona:	Passions:	Preferences:	Principles:
Who the market fundamentally is.	What excites and motivates them?	Their favored choices and patterns.	The beliefs and ethics driving them.

Building Your ICP

Your ICP changes based on who you are targeting. If you are targeting business owners, you will look at firmographics. If you are targeting consumers, you will study demographics. I believe that for either, you should study psychographics. Psychographics is a way of studying people by looking at their thoughts, feelings, and the things they like or do. It helps us understand why people make certain decisions and how they live their lives.

Here is a list of questions you should be able to answer about your target market:

Firmographics (B2B):
- *Company Size:* How many employees does the company have?
- *Industry:* What sector does the company operate in?
- *Revenue:* What is the annual revenue range of this type of business?
- *Location:* Where are such businesses geographically located?

- *Business Model:* What type of business model do they follow (B2B, B2C, etc.)?

Demographics (B2C):
- *Age Range:* What is the age bracket of your ideal customer?
- *Gender:* Which gender(s) does your product/service cater to?
- *Income Level:* What is the typical income range of your customer base?
- *Education:* What level of education do they typically have?
- *Occupation:* What fields or types of jobs do they work in?

Psychographics:
- *Values:* What core values do your customers hold that align with your service?
- *Attitudes:* What are their attitudes towards financial management and growth?
- *Lifestyle:* What kind of lifestyle do they lead, and how does it influence their business decisions?
- *Interests:* What are they interested in outside of work that might intersect with your services?

When you're just starting out, choosing a niche can be highly advantageous. It allows you to identify a specific problem, target a specific market, and address a specific gap within that market. Crafting an Ideal Customer Profile (ICP) helps you customize your product or service to precisely meet the needs of your intended audience.

Problems and Solutions

At the age of 13, I began editing videos for my mom. I edited for a long time until, one day, I got burnt out. I didn't fully grasp the problem I was trying to solve. Instead of editing videos to foster business growth, my main focus was on making money for myself and getting the videos done as quickly as possible so I could get back to my game of Fortnite.

Now I realize that if I had prioritized business growth, it would have had a much greater impact today. Selling a product becomes challenging when you don't understand the solution it provides. That's why it is so crucial to position your product as the desired outcome.

For instance, rather than simply offering video services, it is more effective to sell the idea of bringing in an additional $10k per month for their business. People are not solely interested in video services; they value the increased revenue and time saved through professional editing.

If you want to make a really large sum of money, you must address the problems your customers face. The primary goal of any product is to bridge the gap between the customer's current and desired state.

Start by identifying the key challenges your ideal customers encounter. Make a comprehensive list of these issues and then explore potential solutions. Remember, you need to find their true desire. Most people don't care about the gym; they care about the results they get from it. Solving problems is key to selling your product successfully.

I bridge the gap by identifying a solution that can transition individuals from their current state to their desired state. The bridge could be a tailored fitness program, for example, or a personalized diet plan.

Current State   **Desired State**

Experiment, Evaluate, Iterate

After providing editing services for an extended period, I realized that guaranteeing results for my product was not feasible, so I decided to make some adjustments to my service. I transitioned from the conventional video editing model to the growth marketing model, enabling me to work with companies and help them scale.

Launching a product or service is just the beginning; you must continuously refine it based on feedback and market changes. Split tests are key here so you can enhance customer success. This iterative process ensures that your product or service remains relevant and competitive in the market.

The product and service development process is not a one-time event; it is an ongoing journey. As market trends evolve and customer needs change, adaptation and refinement are vital. Business is all about trial and error, and you must constantly improvise to make your product better.

CHAPTER 3

Branding

In the small yet bustling town of Lake Wylie, a sense of excitement filled the air like the fizz of a freshly opened soda. It was the kind of excitement that only comes with something new and shiny, something that promises fun and delight. For the folks of Lake Wylie, that something was the opening of a new McDonald's. To four-year-old me, this was an adventure waiting to happen.

As I walked through those doors, hand in hand with my parents, my eyes were as wide as burger buns, taking in the kaleidoscope of colors and the buzz of activity. The air was thick with the aroma of fries and burgers, a scent of pure joy. I remember tugging at my mom's hand, urging her to walk faster, my little feet barely keeping up with my excitement.

After ordering, my eagerness came to a sudden halt. There he was, standing taller than anyone else in the room: Ronald McDonald, the iconic clown of the brand. His smile was wide, his hair a fiery red, and his shoes comically large. To everyone else, he was a symbol of happiness and fun, but to my young eyes, he was a giant, startling figure who towered over my tiny world.

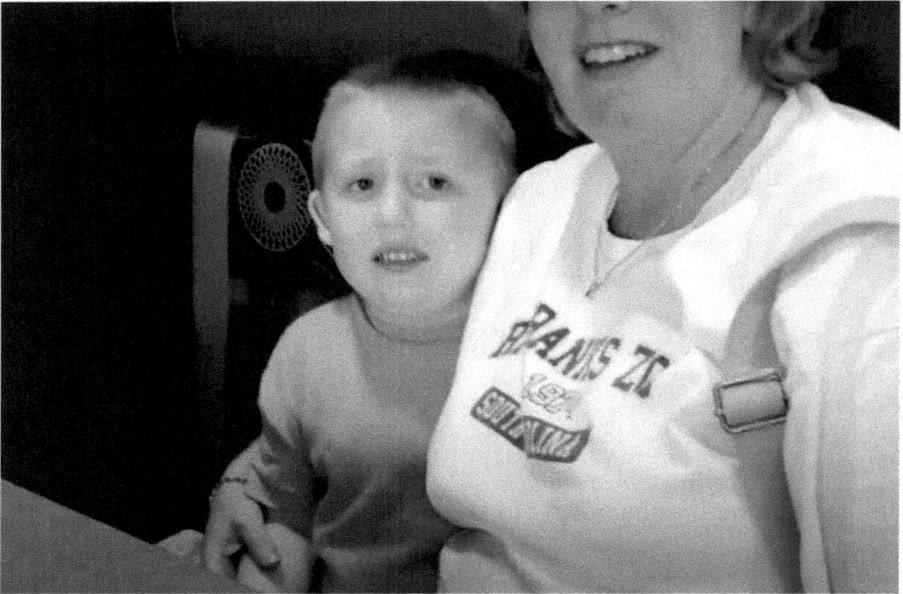

That moment, brief as it was, etched itself into my memory. It was my first real encounter with the power of branding, the moment when I realized that a brand was more than just a name or a logo. A brand, I now understood, was an experience, an emotion, something that could leave an imprint on your heart. I never looked at McDonald's the same way again. The brand that was meant to symbolize joy and fun had, for me, taken on a different shade, one tinged with the unease of that first encounter.

As the years passed, that memory of Ronald McDonald remained vivid in my mind. It taught me how our perceptions are shaped and how a single encounter can color our view of an entire brand.

Since then, I've done a lot of work with branding and worked with a brand coach for a while now. Branding has four core components: positioning, messaging, identity, and experience.

At this point, you may be tempted to move straight into the offer or acquisition and skip branding. People often associate branding with content, and while branding should be used there, it is much more important to have a branded offer. A brand is like the gutter guards in bowling. They keep you headed down a single straight path and prevent any unforced errors of going off-brand.

My brand strategist, Rebecca Gunter, says, "It's like throwing spaghetti against a wall and seeing what sticks vs. knowing your hungry-for-pasta people love marinara made from scratch by Italian grandmothers."

Positioning

I remember it like it was yesterday. I was sitting in my mom's cozy home office, surrounded by notes and a clutter of ideas. My mom, an entrepreneur with a vision for Campground Accounting, her business, had just proposed an exciting project: a podcast that we later named *Campground Compass*. I was thrilled but a little uncertain. How would we make our podcast stand out in the sea of digital content?

That's when I first learned about the concept of "positioning." My mom invited me to participate in a call with Rebecca, who suggested that we position the podcast. The more she talked about it, the more I realized the power of positioning.

I remember sitting down with my mom and explaining my epiphany. "Positioning is like setting up our podcast's tent in the vast campground of the internet," I explained. "We need to pick a spot where we can be seen and heard, where our unique voice and stories resonate with our listeners."

With this newfound understanding, we began shaping *Campground Compass*. We defined our unique angle: a mix of heartfelt family camping stories and expert tips for family-owned campgrounds. Every episode, every story, every tip was filtered through this lens. We were no longer just another camping podcast; we became a go-to resource for campground owners looking to learn more about their businesses.

Positioning typically works in three sessions. The first session is 90 minutes, where you sit down and talk through the actual brand. The second session is for revealing the positioning statement, and the third session is for implementing the positioning.

A positioning statement answers these five questions.

- Who are your people?
- What do they need?
- Who are you?
- What do you deliver?
- Why are you special, different, or the One?

Who Are Your People?

The foundation of a positioning statement starts by pinpointing "your people," often the most challenging part of the process. The key here is to approach this task with a more literal mindset. Use the insights you've gathered from the niche prism exercise. This tool is instrumental in defining the unique segment of the market you aim to serve.

The first step is to deeply analyze their specific challenges and their dream outcomes if they were to get rid of that pain. If you don't know who your people are, you can't align your services with their needs. Consider the limiting beliefs your potential clients might hold. These beliefs could be about the industry, their business capabilities, or even misconceptions about what you offer. Identifying and addressing these beliefs in your positioning statement can significantly enhance its relevance and appeal.

If you find yourself struggling to focus on a single market, shift your perspective to a more personal approach. Ask yourself, "Who do I care about the most?" This introspection can often lead to a clearer understanding of the market segment you are most passionate about serving. Your enthusiasm for helping a particular group can shine through in your positioning statement, making it more authentic and compelling.

In summary, your positioning statement should reflect a thorough understanding of your chosen market segment, uncovered through the niche prism and enriched by your personal passion and insight into the challenges and aspirations of your target audience. This approach will ensure your statement resonates deeply with "your people," setting the foundation for a successful and fulfilling business relationship.

"Who are your people?" is usually the easiest of the five questions to answer. People love to talk about themselves, so you can typically bring some good stuff out of them just by conversing with them. One of the things I look for here is principles. What values do they have? I also want to determine what they know, why they know it, and how they learned it.

What Do They Need?

When we ask, "What does the client need?" we're looking at the essential services that they might need to take themselves or their business to the next level. In my case, I provide the systems and playbooks they need to scale their business.

You also need to answer the question, "Why can't they do it on their own?" What's stopping them?

In the case of a fitness coach, the core offer might be a training program and diet plan, but the person probably won't use them unless they have accountability. Without it, they won't get the result they desire.

What do they *really* want? They don't really want a personal trainer. They want to lose weight. The fitness coach is just the vehicle to get them from their current state to their dream state.

Who Are You?

The next question is, what kind of person are you, or what kind of team do you have? Instead of just thinking about yourself, think about the character of your business. What perception do people have of your business? What characteristics does it have? This is your chance to share what you do.

Here, it is also important to open up about how you relate to your prospective client. Show them that you have gone on the same journey they need to go on and you have been in their shoes.

What Do You Deliver?

The next question is, what do you deliver? What are the logistics of your offer? This can sometimes be hard for people to answer. You need to know how the program or product works to get the client from their current stage to their dream outcome.

The key here is having a good product that takes pain and gives gain. If you can take away pain from the client and give them something to gain, this question will be easy.

How does the product or service get them from their pains to their plans?

Why Are You Special, Different, or the One?

In my experience, "Why are you special, different, or the one?" is either very easy or impossible to answer. I have seen people change their entire business after I asked them this question, and they were right to do so.

When I used to specialize in fitness coaches, this question was almost always left unanswered, but it is the key to success. Every fitness coach offered the same thing: a diet program and a training plan. Some people would tell me, "I offer accountability." This was always funny to me because so does everyone else!

In my opinion, if there is not something unique about your business, you will never be able to reach your dreams because you will always be competing on price. Don't become a commodity.

Why would someone choose you over someone else? Why do you love what you do? Why do you care? A lot of fitness coaches will try to make the exact same offer.

You need to change up your offer a little bit and make it something special that the market hasn't seen before. If you are only offering the same opportunity as everyone else, there's no reason for someone to pick you over your competition.

Finalizing Positioning

After learning about the product, the facilitator will meet to review and validate the positioning statement. Most *normal* copywriters will come back with one positioning statement and assign it.

We are not trying to be normal. We are trying to be the best.

With a positioning statement, I use three versions: the "**Plain Jane**," the "**Gold Standard**," and the "**Vanguard Vision**." Below each is an example I wrote for a new campground sale offer for my mom's accounting firm, Campground Accounting.

The Plain Jane

The Plain Jane version should have a straightforward, no-frills, universally appealing copy. It should be extremely clear and concise, and it should speak to the core values and benefits of the product.

The goal is to be perceived as accessible and dependable and to get the point across without any fluff.

Example: For committed, industrious, and future-focused campground owners who want to get the most bang for their buck without the financial intricacies, [PACKAGE] is the Campground Financial Officer that delivers plans for exit, progressive selling strategies, and promising financial results because if you love your business, you should work on it, not in it.

The Gold Standard

The Gold Standard version should be rich in flavor with a hint of exclusivity and a touch of luxury.

Here, your goal is to craft messages that convey a premium and quality approach and a specialized experience.

> **Example:** For hard-working, down-to-earth, roll-up-your-sleeves campground owners who are Ready to Reinvent, [PACKAGE] is the Campground Wealth Navigator that provides Accounting Acumen, Business Brilliance, and Financial Foresight because life is too short to Focus on Financials and Forget the Fun.

The Vanguard Vision

This version presents the business as cutting-edge, creative, and unafraid of challenges. Here, your goal is to be recognized as a trailblazer and thought leader in your industry.

You want to present yourself as having solutions that challenge the status quo. This approach pushes the boundaries of conventional marketing with innovative and proactive messaging.

I typically use a lot of copy from the Vanguard Vision because I like to be seen as a disruptor in my industry.

> **Example:** For passionate, relentless, and visionary campground owners who are Ready to Reap the Rewards of their Rigorous Routines, [PACKAGE] is the Campground Sale Success Officer that offers peace of mind, untangles the bind, and fortune, you'll find because life is too precious to lose sight of leisure while lost in ledgers.

Putting It All Together

After you have written the three versions, it is time to assemble the final positioning statement. Take pieces of the original positioning statements and build one final draft that you will actually use. Here is an example of my positioning statement for my personal brand:

For ambitious disruptors with unbridled ambition and a well-honed work ethic who will not stand for a life of mediocrity and mindlessness and are ready to pursue potential and 10x their tenacity for personal excellence, Zack Bordeaux is the serial entrepreneur, content creator, and thought leader who delivers the energy, effectiveness, and embodiment of carving out your own path and living on your own terms because grit is grace and destiny isn't determined. You are.

Messaging

Messaging is very simple. It's the stuff you don't use in positioning that is still useful. It's basically just branded copy that is going to get stuck in your head.

You must have a clear and consistent message.

Creating compelling messages that resonate with your target audience is the key to having a recognizable brand.

Brand Identity

Being easily recognizable is huge in the business world. If your logo is just a few circles, it's not going to help your business be recognized. Your logo should tell a story.

Brand identity doesn't just cover the visible elements of your brand, such as color, design, and logo, but also the identities your target market associates with your brand.

When creating a brand identity, you want to create a paradigm shift for your target market from where they are now to where they want to be. To change the way people think about your brand, you have to put them through an identity shift.

Every December, my church (shoutout Elevation) encourages us to pick a word of the year. My word for 2024 was "recreate." Total recreation is the thing amateur entrepreneurs miss. When your client chooses you over the competition, it should have a real effect on their life.

If you offer a service, the best way to change lives is to serve people at the highest level. You need to transfer three emotions into a client:

1. Certainty
2. Energy
3. Expertise

Brand identity is the identity that they shift into after using your service. At the core of every company is the goal of creating an experience that the target market will love. This means going beyond the product and communicating on a deeper level with clients.

If you haven't already, I recommend starting a movement. You want your people to feel that they belong to a community. When I built DozerDog, my movement portrayed a group of killers with a dogged mindset who could bulldoze through and destroy the competition. Consequently, my fans became very loyal to my brand because it stood for something my ICP believed in.

Three things affect people's perception of a brand: *voice, values,* and *visuals.*

Voice

In this day and age, people want personality. People don't buy from business brands on social media anymore; they buy from personal brands.

You can probably tell who most people are just by the way they talk or write a text, right? That's because they have a unique way of speaking that's instantly recognizable.

Brand voice refers to the emotion and personality the brand conveys when communicating. So, are you angry? Are you fired up? Are you more toned down? How do you present yourself? What tone of voice do you use?

The brand voice can be professional, friendly, authoritative, humorous, or any other adjective you can think of. The language of your brand is not just Spanish or English but the specific words and idioms you use, as well as the jargon of your market.

Each piece of communication should have a clear and concise purpose. Whether it's to inform, entertain, persuade, or some combination of these three, knowing why you're communicating makes it a lot easier to decide what you're going to say and how to say it. This is where you need to have a vision for your company and a mission statement. It also ensures that your communication is always relevant to your audience and you always have something to say. That way, you always are dialed in on who your people are.

Values

Creating core values that genuinely define your brand requires understanding that these principles must hold significance for you and your target audience. They should resonate on two levels: internally (within your business) and externally (with your customers). But how can you craft such values? I have developed a methodology: the "**Specific Seven Formula**."

The Specific Seven Formula emphasizes that each of your core values should be specific, well-defined, and more than just a single word. While a one-word value like "leadership" may seem appealing due to its simplicity, it's too abstract and open to multiple interpretations, diluting its effectiveness in communicating what you truly stand for.

Instead, your core values should be action statements, offering a more comprehensive and concrete representation of your brand's ethos. For instance, take "lead by example" as a core value. It is specific, meaningful, and leaves little room for ambiguity, making it a far more potent representation of your commitment to leadership.

To build a brand that resonates with you and your audience, it's important to first internalize your core values. These values should reflect your beliefs and principles and should be embraced not only by you but also by your entire team. Merely stating these values is not enough; they need to be embodied in all the team's actions, decisions, and interactions.

Communication of these values is equally important. They should be clearly and consistently expressed across all platforms to help your target market understand what your brand stands for. These core values must align with the beliefs and expectations of your target audience. Such alignment increases the chances of building strong, lasting relationships with them.

Core values should influence business decisions, whether it's hiring a new team member or launching a new product. As your brand evolves, revisit these values regularly to ensure they still accurately represent your brand. In times of conflict, these core values can provide a clear path to resolution.

Forcing adherence to your core values is crucial, and one effective way to do this is to recognize and reward actions that embody these values. Regular reinforcement keeps these values at the forefront of everyone's minds, ensuring they remain an integral part of your brand's identity.

Here are my core values below:

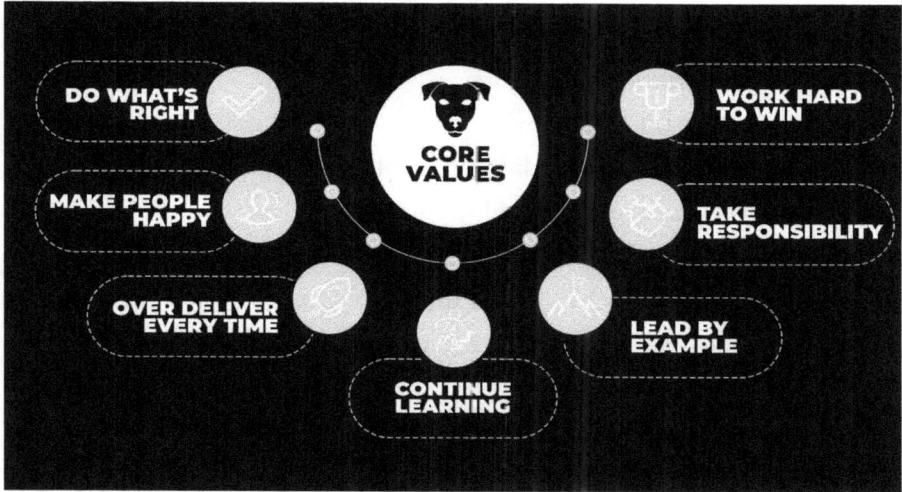

Visuals

Visuals don't just mean your logo but also your colors, typography, and imagery. This is where building a brand style guide comes in handy. The assets you use on a regular basis need to be organized, well thought out, and specific to your brand. This varies for every business, but you should make a list of dos and don'ts for your brand. For example, I never use visuals of people in suits and ties, paper, or calculators in my brand visuals because they don't fit the people I am trying to target

Brand Experience

As my family pulled into the Ohio campground, rain poured from the sky like a waterfall over a cliff. After arriving, my mom grabbed her rain jacket and ventured out to the entrance of the camp store. The door creaked open, and she stepped into the building.

Her mission was simple: get checked into the campground so we could get to the site and out of the rain as quickly as possible.

But that's not how things panned out.

"The official check-in time is 3:00 p.m.," the woman behind the counter stated with a smug look on her face. "Currently, it is 1:20 p.m., so I'm adding a $45 early check-in fee to your balance."

My mom questioned the fee, pointing out that the site was unoccupied. Why charge for a service that didn't disrupt anyone? The worker, however, was as immovable as a towering redwood, insistent on adhering to the policy.

Rules are rules, so my mom said that was fine, but she would mention it in the review. From out of nowhere, the lady started screaming and said we were threatening her. She ended up kicking us out of the campground.

What this lady didn't know is that my mom is the owner of Campground Accounting and has a very large influence in the campground community. My mom made a YouTube video about the interaction to teach campground owners what not to do in that situation. It was the top-performing video we have ever posted on the channel. Over 45,000 people have seen it at the time of writing this book. While we didn't mention exactly what campground it was, we could have, and people would have had a bad impression of that campground.

We Got Kicked Out of a Campground!
47K views · 4 months ago >100x

Campground Accounting

We share a jaw-dropping RV travel horror story where we were unexpectedly kicked out of a campground Join us as we ...

Customer experience directly influences your brand's reputation, which is an integral part of your brand itself. You need to map out a seamless customer journey, from onboarding to the final interaction with your company.

1st Phorm is a supplement company that is a great example of how to do this right. If you have ever ordered something from 1P, you know that they provide an incredible customer experience. They send personalized handwritten notes with their packages.

Great customer experience helps make people loyal to the brand. Even if you don't have the skills to be the best at the service you are delivering, you can still be the best at customer service. Putting customer experience before profit will help ensure that you hit your goals.

I treat my clients as if we are friends, and they become extremely loyal to me and my brand. Such a strategy is especially important when you are a beginner. Put your clients' best interests first, and you will never have a money problem.

CHAPTER 4

Offer

As I was growing up, we always had a landscaper come to our house. My mom would tell me how cheap he was and that he should ask for a raise. Over the course of 10 years, he never asked for a raise.

This was a very valuable lesson for me. I learned that if I want to make more money, I have to ask. A lot of times, people are willing to give you more money than you would think.

Closed mouths don't get fed.

Over the years, labor has gotten more expensive. Raising your prices is a natural process that people expect. Business owners know that if the landscaper had just asked for more money, he would have gotten it.

If you provide a quality service, you're going to have a lot more leverage when asking for that price raise. One big problem that I see a lot of people making is undervaluing themselves.

Are you your own target market?

Are you the person who is buying your product?

Often, the answer is no, yet people still base their willingness to buy off their own opinions.

For example, I'm not an online coach, but I might sell a product to them. I shouldn't make assumptions about what online coaches want without first getting the opinion of an actual online coach.

I am not my own target market, so I need to stop undervaluing myself and perceiving myself as less than I actually am.

When I was in college, I started drinking Fiji water. From the first sip, I knew that it was of a higher quality than other bottled waters and had a higher value. What really makes people value Fiji water is the high price point.

Although it's just water, the more it costs, the more value it seems to provide.

The higher the perceived value, the more people are willing to pay.

As a result, if you charge more, people are going to perceive your product or service as more valuable.

There's no benefit to being the lowest price. If you don't watch out, you might just win the race to the bottom.

But there is a huge benefit to being the highest priced because you're going to be seen as the industry leader, providing the most valuable service.

There are four types of products, and they all have different buying triggers:

- **Luxuries** are bought because people want status. A luxury is an expensive want.
- **Trinkets** are bought on impulse. A trinket is a cheap want.
- **Commodities** are bought based on price. A commodity is a cheap need.
- **Necessities** are bought due to force. A necessity is an expensive need.

Want

Luxury	Trinket

Need

Necessity	Commodity
	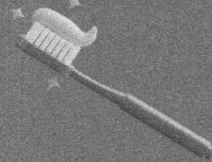

Expensive Cheap

The big idea here is that everything people buy most things is based on emotion.

Logic doesn't sell—*emotion* does.

If you're currently providing a commodity, the easiest way to get out of that category is to add status. When you do, your product becomes a luxury.

Creating an Offer That Prints

What does a printing offer mean? It means that the offer has a return on advertising spend (ROAS)—if you put $1 in and get $2 out, that offer "prints" money.

The goal is to make an infinite money machine. There are four principles to crafting a high-converting offer: it needs to be quick, easy, have huge potential for growth, and have a high likelihood of producing results.

Quick

Time to first value (TTFV) is one of the most important aspects of an offer. We'll get more into onboarding later, but for now, just remember that after a prospect buys a service, they regret their purchase more and more as time goes on.

The quicker you can bring them value, the more they're going to like your product. You need to implement a quick result and a long-term result. The quick result ensures that they don't regret their purchase, and the long term result provides them with something bigger than they could have ever imagined.

Your goal should be to leap your customers over the competition and turn decades into days. The quicker you get results, the happier the client will be.

Easy

Think about the amount of effort and sacrifice the client has to make to get where they want to go.

The more value that you put into a product, the more people are willing to pay for it.

Value vs Price Willingness

The harder it is to fulfill a product, the easier it is to sell that product. The easier it is to fulfill a product, the harder it is to sell that product. If it is more difficult to fulfill, the value is higher because if people wanted to fulfill it on their own, it would take more effort and sacrifice.

Fulfillment Ease vs Difficulty of Sale

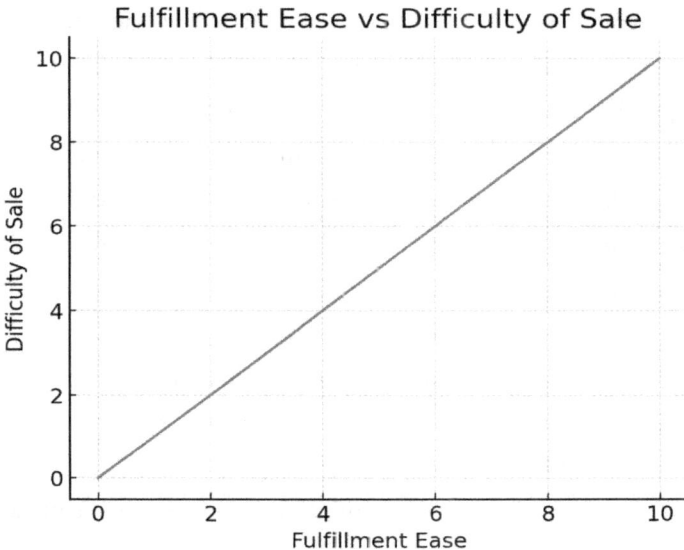

Potential

How much potential value does your offer have? What are the potential downsides? Think back to the decision-making matrix from earlier. If I could make you $10,000, how much would that be worth? Well, for most people, they would be willing to put in $1,000 to get $10,000 out. A lot of people buy off potential and how much they can potentially get out of something.

You also have to think of the downsides. If a prospect has to take on a lot of risk to get the result they want, they are a lot less likely to take advantage of your offer. If you take some of the weight off of their shoulders, they will add some weight to your wallet. What is the worst-case scenario, and what's the best-case scenario?

Offer Launches

My career is over, I thought as I stared at my Stripe account. The balance read *$0.00*. I had spent the last six months getting ready to launch a new business model called Optimize Oasis. Just three days before, I had just lost two of my highest-paying clients, but I wasn't worried because I knew this new model would be a success. My vision faded at the snap of a finger. Optimize Oasis was a complete failure.

It flopped because I didn't prepare for the launch correctly. When I launched the offer, all I did was send an email to the 27 people on my email list (most of whom didn't care about my offer). Some people were already interested in the offer, but I didn't actually develop the systems to launch it.

However, instead of just giving up, I went back to the drawing board and rebranded the model as DozerDog Development.

I rebranded the product in a way that made people feel better about the product because it could draw on the track record of DozerDog Designs, which had been around for four years at this point.

If your product fails, the reason might just be the way it's presented.

After this giant failure, I began to study how the greatest of the greats do offer launches. After much trial and error, I have finally found something that works: an evergreen framework that can be adapted to any platform or niche. The SPARK framework is my proven method for creating successful offer launch campaigns: signal, promote, activate, revenue, and kindle.

Step 1: Signal

The first thing you want to do is signal the upcoming release of the big project. This is going to build anticipation and create a sense of intrigue. The goal is to allude to the product or service and give the idea that you're working on something big. Don't state what the product actually is, but tell people that you're working on something special for them. This will build suspense on the front end.

Step 2: Promote

Next, you want to promote. You want to spend the last three days before you launch the product promoting things such as free guides. This could involve sharing snippets, testimonials, templates, or other engaging content from your product. The goal is to get micro-commitments and build rapport before you actually launch the product.

Step 3: Activate

The third step is to activate. This is when you launch the offer using reveals and story sequences to captivate your audience. The idea here is to plan the launch in advance. The more stuff that you can do on that date, the better. You should be using different mediums and repurposing the launch for multiple platforms.

Step 4: Revenue

Once your offer is live, it's time to generate some revenue. After you have accepted some orders and the cash is rolling in, the goal is to get enough revenue to fund some ads.

Step 5: Kindle

Finally, we want to enhance our reach and sales by kindling the interest through targeted ads. So, we're going to use some cash flow from Organic and reinvest it into some ads. From there, we'll monitor the ads and adjust them for optimal results.

With Optimize Oasis, I messed up big time because I was trying to do a full launch and no one bought. Consequently, I didn't get any revenue in and couldn't kindle the offer. This meant I couldn't scale the offer. No bueno.

Offer Stacks

One of the biggest advantages of my business is that I offer a large stack of value. I don't just offer one thing; I offer a lot of different products built up inside of an offer stack. I never lower my prices; I only increase value. For example, in my current offer stack, I'm not just offering one thing. I have a lot of different bonuses and add-ons that come inside of that package: business consulting, done-for-you content, sales systems, a course, copy-and-paste resources, backend systems, etc.

You also need to make sure that your offer is limited and time sensitive. This will add an incentive for people to buy *now* versus waiting until later. Speed is king.

Guarantees

I used to be scared of guaranteeing my product because I worried that it wouldn't produce a result for my clients. This is when I realized that the guarantee was not my problem; the product was my problem.

If your product isn't good enough to get a result, there's a good chance you shouldn't be selling it. Now, in some rare cases, there are legal issues where you're not able to actually sell a result, but in most cases, guarantees are not going to hurt you.

I would try to explain all this myself, but I believe millionaire entrepreneur and bestselling author Alex Hormozi sums it up best in his book *$100M Offers*. He explains that if you have a hundred sales with a 5% refund rate, you will end up with 95 net sales. If introducing a guarantee increases your sales to 130 with 13 refunds, a 10% refund rate—double the original amount—you will have 117 net sales. This approach results in a 23% increase in sales over the long term. While there's a concern that people might take advantage of the guarantee, the focus shouldn't be on the number of refunds but on the bottom line. When you understand this, you realize that guarantees are among the strongest strategies a business can implement. The key is ensuring you can fulfill them.

CHAPTER 5

Outbound Leads

The biggest pain point for most online business owners is getting clients. Without clients, there is no business.

But the truth is, getting leads doesn't have to be a complicated and stressful process. With the right strategies and tactics, you can easily attract high-quality leads and convert them into paying customers.

The hardest part about this chapter is keeping the information evergreen. There are thousands of ways to go about finding leads, and everyone will tell you their way is best. Everyone is right and wrong.

The best way to acquire leads is whichever method you can stick to long term. If you can't send DMs daily, it probably isn't the best system for you. If you don't have any money, paid ads probably aren't for you.

The big idea you will hear throughout this chapter is to do what other people don't do and get the results other people won't get.

The truth is, any system can work wonders if you work to make it happen. This chapter will cover all of the ways you can acquire customers. The important thing is not that you do all of them but that you make a commitment to stick to one of them for a long time. I recommend you do it every day for at least a year.

The Acquisition Equation

$$(\text{Inbound} + \text{Outbound})(\text{Cold} + \text{Warm})$$

The first thing that I look at whenever I'm developing an acquisition strategy is the acquisition equation. In eighth-grade math class, you probably learned how to multiply polynomials. This is the same concept.

The three types of traffic are **warm traffic, hot traffic,** and **cold traffic.** The warmer your prospects are, the more likely they are to know about your product.

- **Warm traffic** refers to those who are already aware of your brand, product, or service. These individuals have had some level of interaction with your company.

- **Hot traffic** consists of your fans who love what you are doing. They are aware of your product, your company, and you. They have most likely already purchased from you in the past.

- **Cold traffic** is made up of all the strangers who don't know about your stuff. They are new prospects who have never heard of you, your product, or your company. These are typically harder to sell because they don't have any rapport with you yet.

There are two types of traffic sources: **inbound and outbound**. These terms sound technical, I know, but believe me when I say they're integral to understanding the dynamics of your online presence.

- **Inbound traffic** is like your open house party, where everyone is invited. It refers to visitors who land on your website organically, perhaps through search engines, social media shares, or word-of-mouth recommendations. If you are not reaching out to these people, they are inbound traffic. These folks found you because they were looking for something specific that aligns with what you offer.

- **Outbound traffic** is a bit more aggressive. It's like knocking on doors in an unfamiliar neighborhood while trying to sell vacuum cleaners. Outbound traffic involves reaching out directly to potential customers through paid advertising methods such as pay-per-click ads or cold DMs. Basically, it is your effort to go out into the cold streets of the internet to find users who may not be aware of your brand yet and draw them into the warmth of your product or service offering.

In his bestselling book *The 48 Laws of Power*, Robert Greene says, "MAKE OTHER PEOPLE COME TO YOU—USE BAIT IF NECESSARY: When you force the other person to act, you are the one in control. It is always better to make your opponent come to you, abandoning his own plans in the process. Lure him with fabulous gains—then attack. You hold the cards." Inbound traffic will always be easier to sell & deliver on because they are interested in the service.

Evergreen Acquisition

Marketing changes every day. What worked yesterday won't work today. As I mentioned earlier, the biggest challenge in creating this book is keeping the information evergreen. I want this book to work and be applicable in a hundred years (if the world still exists).

While some of the specific tactics may change, one concept always holds true: saturation is the killer of quality clients.

If you only take one thing from this book, it should be this critical concept for acquiring customers: do what others don't and get the results others won't.

If something is easy, it probably won't get you results. When you do challenging things, you create an opportunity to build your mindset.

The easiest way to acquire clients is by doing the hardest things that no one else is willing to do.

For example, most people are not willing to film personalized cold video emails and manually find information for leads.

Personalization has a cap on quantity. Most people will say it's not efficient. What is efficient is not what is easiest. What is efficient is what works. I can tell you right now that everyone tries to take the easy route. That's why everyone fails.

Your goal should be to serve your clients at the highest level. This means going out of your way to actually care about them.

Cold Outbound – Calls, Emails, Messages

Soon after I started my growth partner business, one of my mentors said to me, "Do you think you're gonna attract the big guys through AI and automation?" I realized that if I wanted to be a big player, then I had to be a big player. In other words, if I wanted big deals, I had to put in big effort.

I believe your cold outreach should be personalized every time so that you stand out from the crowd. Eighty percent of people use the exact same script. When you steal it, you look like a dork in a sea of NPCs. Create your own frameworks and be unique.

My system for cold outbound is called the **FIND Framework.** It involves a series of steps to effectively engage with potential customers.

FIND stands for:

F – Foster context and familiarity.

I – Identify inefficiencies and qualify.

N – Narrate the best way (your process/solution).

D – Determine availability (book a call).

To foster context and familiarity, you have to build rapport quickly. This will help build trust right from the start. The more people trust you, the more likely they are to actually buy from you in the future, so you must build trust very quickly.

Using humor is a good strategy because it's what you would do if you were talking to a friend. The phrase "make a friend, make a sale" is kind of cliché, but everyone uses it for a reason: it works.

Next up, you need to identify the pain points and inefficiencies in the prospect's current way of attempting to solve their core problem.

You don't want to tell them their pain points; help them realize what they are on their own. Make it their idea every time. This will also help you qualify and see if they're actually a good fit for your service or if you should just give them a lead magnet.

Next, narrate the best way to get rid of the pain. This is where you bring out your process/method for fixing the pain they feel and helping them get to where they want to go. Identify what their dream outcome is and how you can help them get closer to it.

One of my biggest character flaws is overcomplicating things. I have a very systemized mindset, so I tend to make things more complicated than they need to be. Doing this makes the prospect think that you're less qualified than you actually are. Don't over explain; keep it simple and straight to the point.

The last step is to book the prospect for a call. Once they're interested, send them a calendar link or whatever you're trying to sell.

DM setting should be a step of your funnel, nudging the prospect closer to buying your product. You should map out the customer journey and build your script around it.

How Many Outreaches Should You Do?

"DMs don't work," I told one of my mentors when I was first getting into the marketing space. "How many messages do you think I should be sending?"

Instead of telling me to send the typical hundred outbound messages per day, he asked me, "Well, how many do you think you should be sending?"

Whatever your answer to this question is, it is probably low, but you should send at least that many. What I would recommend is, if you don't have a client yet, spend four to six hours a day on sending DMs. If you already have some clients, testimonials, and leverage, you should be spending less time on it.

The more time you spend sending messages, the more people you get in the door. Look at what other people are doing and do way more. When everyone else is sending a hundred DMs, my team is sending four hundred to five hundred every day.

Warm Outbound – Retargeting

Most people waste 90% of their quality lead flow by not retargeting the leads that are engaging with them. When you have a warm audience, you should engage with them consistently. The beauty of retargeting is that you don't have to constantly worry about where you're going to find leads.

My strategy for retargeting is called **Organic Engagement Amplification Retargeting**. Most people just make content and hope leads will flow in. This does not work for 99% of people and you will leave money on the table that should *not* be your strategy. You need to be touching base with your audience.

You should be having conversations with any person who engages with your content and looks like they could be potentially qualified leads. If you are on social media, use DMs. A quick trick I learned with email is to collect emails and phone numbers and then give them a call whenever they fill out the form.

Retargeting allows you to keep your brand top-of-mind for those who have already shown interest in your content.

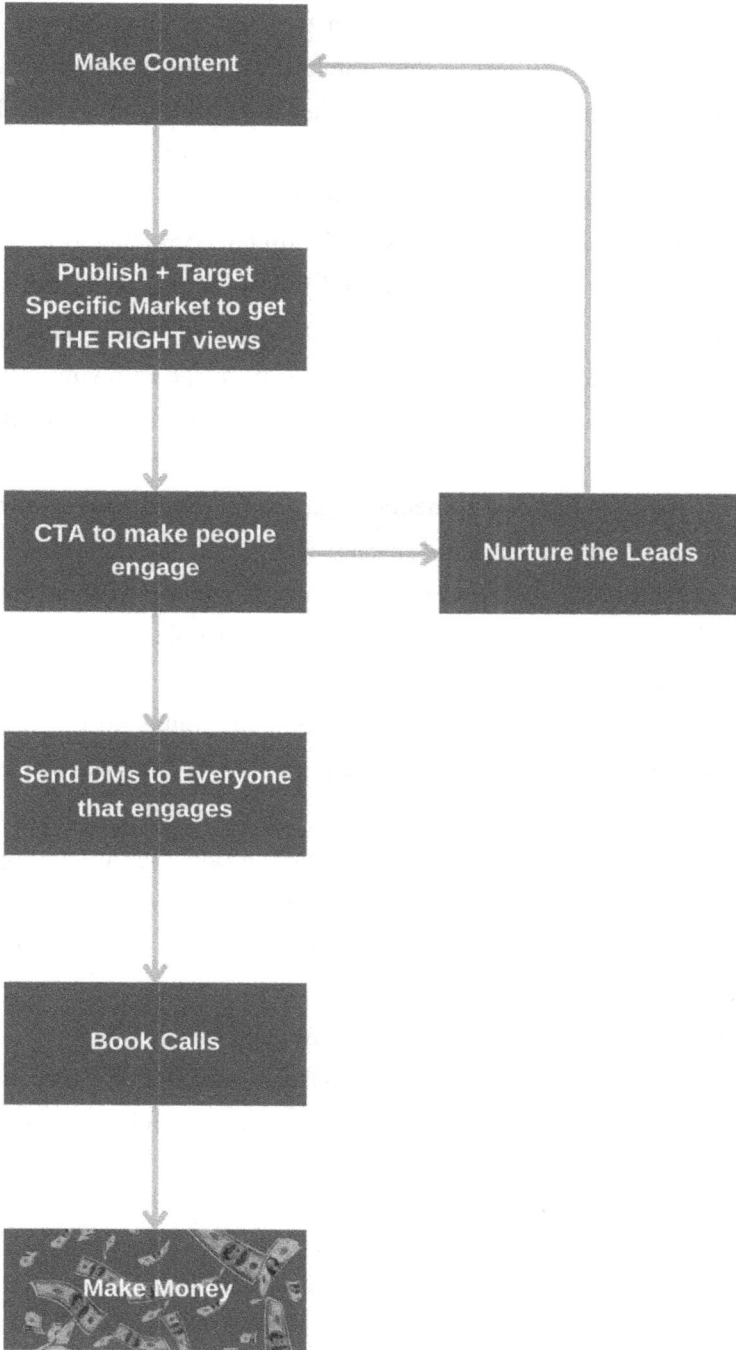

If you have followed all the steps in the content chapter, your videos should give viewers an ROI when they watch them. When you publish a video, make sure you're targeting the right market to get the right views. There's nothing worse than having the wrong audience on your account.

I've worked with many fitness coaches whose entire audience consisted of people who were already into fitness and didn't need a coach. I worked with one guy who had two hundred thousand followers and could not get one client because he had that same problem. At the end of these videos, you can add calls to action (CTAs) to tell your viewers to engage with you.

The next step is actually retargeting people. Every time someone likes, comments, shares, or does any sort of action related to your content, you need to retarget them. Whenever someone engages, they're already a warm and interested lead, so it's often an easier sale.

To make money, you need to book calls. If you are making outbound calls, the first is probably going to involve giving people something for free. It's not a sales call, so don't treat it like one.

The actual way you make money is by providing value. Reciprocity is key. Make sure that after you make a call, you study it to find out ways to improve the next one.

If you don't have a client yet and are taking calls that are ending in no closes, you should review each and every one of them to see what the problem is. Once you have identified your bottleneck, it's going to be a lot easier to continue to grow.

Now comes the fun part: making the money.

After you start making money, don't get comfortable. Keep booking calls. Once you scale the business, you can get a setter, and they can do all of that for you.

CHAPTER 6

Inbound Leads – Content

Growing up, I always dreamed of becoming a YouTuber. I turned that dream into a reality when I uploaded my first video on Aug 5, 2013. Now, the content wasn't great (in fact, some may consider it horrible), but I did gain my passion for content.

Content takes many forms. I define content as a piece of information that is presented through media. While there are many forms of content, the basics of content will almost never change

Niches Don't Get Riches

In the world of business, the niche is the most important thing you can have. If you don't know who you are selling to, you can't sell anything. But content is not about selling.

Content is about building authority and making people respect you. When you have authority, you instantly give people a reason to follow you. The goal with content is to catch people's attention and get them through the door. Content is still at the top of the funnel.

Your content should be broad and personal. As we see a rise in AI, people are going to want to connect with humans more than ever. Personal brands are a must because they are the easiest way to build a deep connection with the audience right from the start.

I use an 80/20 rule here: 80% of my content is about broad topics that don't really directly relate to my business or my brand, and 20% of my content is niched down. Virality and attention are the goals of content.

Think about it. Are you more likely to buy from someone who reaches out to you with a hundred followers or someone with a hundred thousand followers? The obvious answer is the person with a hundred thousand because they have more trust behind them.

Having more followers often leads to more trust. However, many content creators give up and say the algorithm does not favor their content. News flash for you: the platform has the leverage, not you. You don't have the luxury of the algorithm favoring you unless you favor the algorithm.

Let's reverse engineer the algorithm of every platform. The ultimate goal of the platform is to make money. Most platforms make money through paid ads. For paid ads to work, the platform needs two things to fall in place. First, they need to have a good ratio of free content to ads, or people will click away. They also need to have enough people on the platform actively engaging with the content to see the ads.

So, how do we favor the algorithm? Well, it's simple. We create highly engaging, consumable content that viewers watch all the way to the end. The algorithm wants viewers to stay on the platform. The longer someone spends watching your video, the more ads the platform can show them. Watch time is the most important metric.

All content is made of many micro-components. Each of these content components has three parts: a hook, suspense, and value.

The hook is the part at the beginning of a content component that gets the viewer ready to consume. Most people have short attention spans, so it is important to make a bold claim, foreshadow value, and ask a question to grab their attention.

The suspense is the middle part of the content component, where you build up anticipation and keep the viewer engaged. If the content doesn't make the viewer want to continue watching, they will scroll away. And if they scroll away, there goes your watch time.

You must end with value. If you don't deliver on your promise from the hook, viewers will feel disappointed and not actually engage with the content. The best way to do this is by giving actionable advice that viewers can act on immediately.

Content can come in many different forms, so it can be hard to decide what types you should create. I think all types are valuable, but the biggest levers to pull are the ones that are the most engaging.

I like videos for two reasons. For one thing, making videos is the easiest for me to stay consistent with. I have a hard time sitting down and writing content for long periods of time. The second and real reason I like video is because it is currently the most consumed type of content on the market. The less friction your viewers have to get through to watch your videos, the more likely they are to watch them.

After owning a video marketing agency, I learned all of the steps to streamlining a video process. Now I teach people how to build in-house agencies. Agencies are typically very expensive. The good news is that you can build the same systems in your business.

The goal is to take as much friction out of the process as possible. Ideally, you only need to plan the ideas, record the video, and upload it. Outsource all of the low-leverage tasks like video editing and thumbnail design.

After you record the video, you can upload it to a cloud-based storage platform where the editor can find it and download it. I like to store all of mine in Google Drive because it is the easiest for my team to work with.

Once the video is uploaded, Zapier, an automation platform, automatically sends a message to the chat for my Slack channel so my editors can start working on it. This also tells my thumbnail designer to start making the thumbnail.

Next, the video is edited and uploaded to a platform we use called Frame.io for revisions. Frame.io allows me to review each video frame by frame. I manually review all of my videos. For a short time, I had a creative director who reviewed them for me, but I enjoy watching my own videos back and analyzing them. If you just record and post them without analysis, you will never get better at your craft.

Once the revisions are done, the final video is uploaded to Google Drive, which I can download and then upload to my social media pages.

After talking with many of the big dawgs in the industry, I realized that post schedulers are killing people's growth. External scheduling platforms will make you look like a robot on the social media platform because you post on the hour and because bots use external apps through the platforms API.

Platforms want their customers to have the best experience possible because the happier their customers are, the more ads they can show and the more money they can make. If there are robots on the platform, it decreases the customer experience. You should manually post everything to your social media. You can find a social media manager to do this for you, but make sure they are located in the same area as you and share the same time zone.

Currently, I manually post everything I do because I write long, thoughtful captions on each of my posts. The goal of your caption should be to bring value to your target market. Most people just put a stupid motivational quote. I write a full caption that is multiple lines long. Here is an example of what a caption looks like for one of my posts:

I use Apple Notes to come up with ideas for my captions. I keep a long list of one-liners and thoughts there. Whenever I go to the gym, as I warm up on the treadmill, I will write a caption. I don't always use the caption because I don't post every day, but I always have captions ready at a moment's notice. There are no copywriting secrets that I use. I genuinely just spill out my thoughts and organize them in the most efficient way possible.

The Story Formula

I use the same style on my Instagram stories. Instagram stories are the backbone of my social media strategy. They are a place to share my life with my viewers. My posts are not scripted or even very professional, for that matter.

Serial Entrepreneur and bestselling author Gary Vaynerchuk (Gary Vee) talks a lot about documenting as opposed to creating. If you are really about this life, you should be able to document your life and have a cool story to tell. Throughout the day, I take pictures of everything I do. I have many terabytes of photos and videos in my iCloud of my day-to-day life. I also have an agreement with my friends that whenever we see each other doing something that looks badass, we take videos and pictures. If you have friends like this, you are unstoppable.

Posts help you grow; stories build rapport. Rapport is the reason people buy from a personal brand. People want to buy from people, not a logo.

You should post stories **five to eight times per day**. I know most of you just read that and are wondering how you could even post three times a day. If you overcomplicate stories, you will never be able to make one that people will want to watch. Your stories should be authentic. That means you shouldn't be planning them out. You should just make them when the time comes.

Stories are not supposed to be extravagant productions. They should be simple. I generally use five story formats: knowledge posts, talking-head posts, lifestyle footage, promo stores, and post promotions. The chart below shows how much they should be used in proportion to each other. Note that these are not all of the possible story formulas, just the most common ones I use.

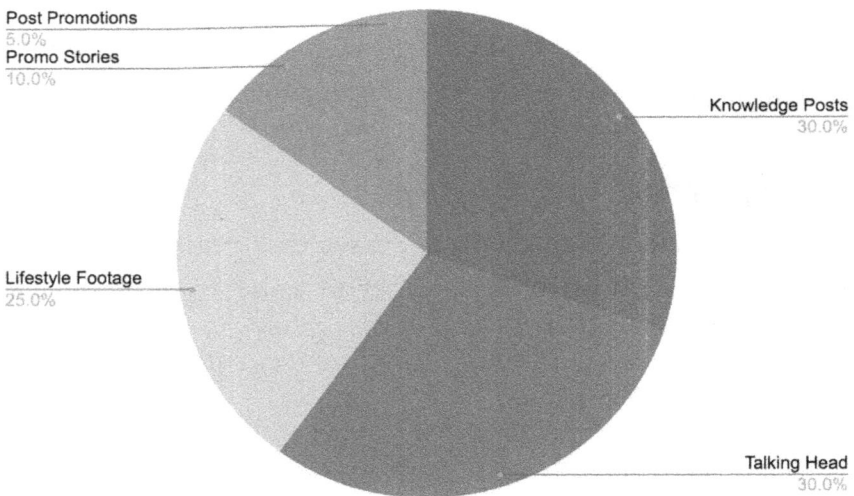

Post Promotions
5.0%
Promo Stories
10.0%
Knowledge Posts
30.0%
Lifestyle Footage
25.0%
Talking Head
30.0%

Knowledge Posts (30%)

If you are treating your personal brand as a business, you should be trying to provide as much value as possible to your audience. The easiest way to provide value is to give your audience some secret sauce.

In this type of post, I typically start with a lifestyle photo or video in the background (more on this in a minute). I then lower the exposure to make it a bit darker and cleaner. There are four ways to do this.

- **Apple Photos:** If you tap the screen (while taking the picture), you can lower the exposure to the desired level.

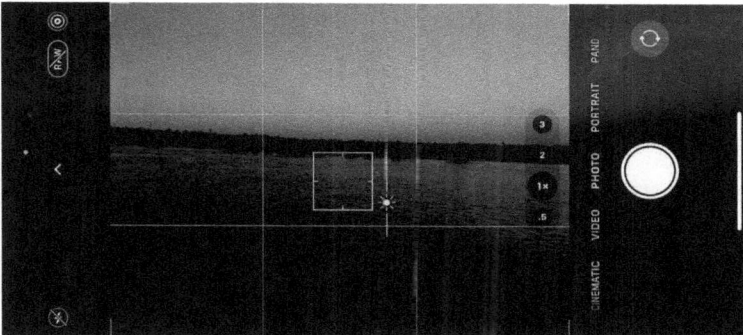

- **Apple Photos (after taking picture):** Go to "Edit" and press "Exposure." Lower the exposure by swiping to the left until the number is negative.

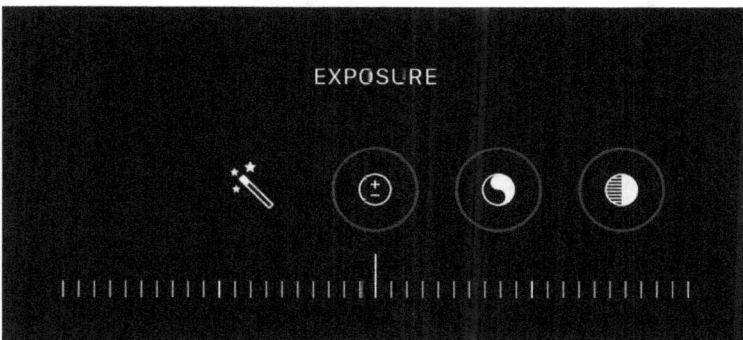

- **Adobe Lightroom:** Once you open your photo in LR, go to "Lighting" and then "Exposure" and turn it down. Check the tutorial in the resource library.

- **Instagram filters:** you can use an Instagram filter after you import everything into your story. Sometimes, they work; sometimes, they don't. Watch your video and make sure it doesn't glitch out, which can sometimes happen with these.

After you have darkened your lifestyle footage, you can add some of your brain. Your knowledge is your most valuable resource, so make sure you show it off. The more you give, the more you get.

I typically add a few lines of text in the same format that I would write a Tweet with. I want it to be a few sentences on different lines with a space between them. Make sure that you use your space wisely. Don't repeat words.

Repetitiveness makes people click on to the next story. Make sure that each sentence can stand alone and still make sense.

I always end with a bang. The ending should be something that sparks interest. In the example below, I used "The stress is the best" as my closing sentence.

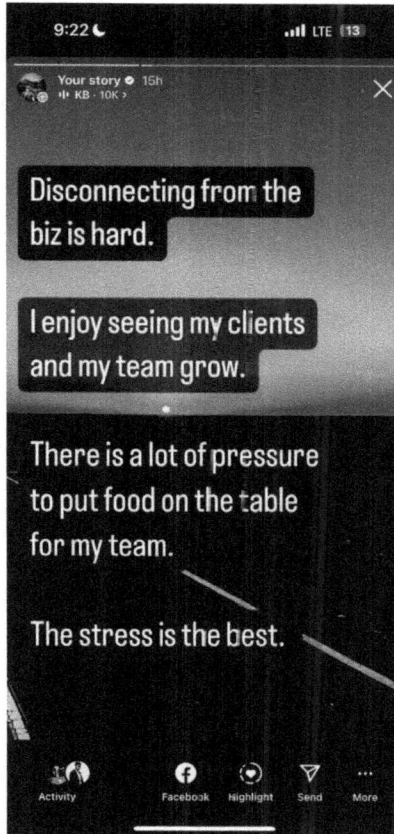

Don't make the post too long. Three to six lines is ideal. If it is too long, people will skip through, and it will decrease your watch time (therefore decreasing the amount of people who actually stay for your content).

Ideally, this lifestyle footage will have you in it, but that is not always possible. I like to post photos and videos that are more recent. In the example above, I took the photo on a bus tour in Egypt. I immediately color-corrected my image in Lightroom, picked my song, and wrote the text to go with it. Again, stories should not take you a long time to make. This story took me around three minutes from ideation to publication.

Talking Head (30%)

Talking-head footage (aka head to camera) is one of the best forms of engaging your fans because they can see you and what you do on a daily basis. I usually try to give one to three pro tips every day through my stories. These usually contain the same type of information that I use in my knowledge stories, just explained via talking instead of written text.

Like I said before, people buy from people. You want to show your authentic self to your audience. Talk to them about what you are going through. Documenting your life (via any medium) is the easiest way to get content.

Just put your phone up and talk directly to the camera. Guess what?—it will not be perfect. When I first started, I made a rule for myself that said that I could only do the video in one take. If I messed up, I still had to post it. Soon, you will no longer mess up. The only way to get better on camera is to get on camera and practice.

For this kind of story, you can consider background music, but it is not necessary. Just make sure that if there is background music, the song doesn't overshadow what you're saying and doesn't have lyrics in it. You can easily add captions in the Instagram app.

Lifestyle Footage (25%)

Capturing lifestyle footage is one of the most important concepts when it comes to posting stories. I consider lifestyle footage a compound asset because it can be used in so many ways. Unlike most videos, it can be reused.

Lifestyle footage can be many things. Here are 10 things you can shoot:

1. Typing on a computer/working.
2. Eating/food.
3. Sitting inside a car, getting into a car, or a panoramic view of your car.
4. Talking in meetings.
5. Videos of you filming (side angle of a head-to-camera video).
6. Dogs or pets.
7. Working out.
8. Scenery.
9. Hobbies.
10. Whatever else fits your brand.

The easiest way to capture lifestyle footage is with a tripod. You can buy them for cheap on Amazon. You don't have to have the most expensive tripod; you just need one that works. If you have someone to film for you (hired or friend), you can get some great shots that have movement.

When I started recording this kind of footage, I realized how easy recording can be. You shouldn't try to think of things to record. Change your mindset. You should record the things you already do on a daily basis. Documenting instead of recording is the way you create a media machine.

Results Stories (10%)

You should be doing promotions often, but not in the traditional sense of just promoting your product. Promotional posts should showcase results. I found it easiest to write case studies and promote them in my story. Showcasing results will add more social proof. If you don't have any results to show, DO NOT promote your product/service.

People hate to be spammed, and bullshit detectors are higher than ever nowadays. Never promote your product by just posting a picture of it or telling people you are open to work. That is how you get unfollowed. People don't want to buy products. They want to buy the desired outcome of the products. They buy off of emotion, not logic. The emotional thought that you should be bringing them is either them making more money or wasting less time.

Post Promotions (CTAs) (5%)

Promoting your posts is not super important, and generally, it won't change the growth you get, but it is sometimes still a good way to get out an extra story. Instead of just putting the post on my story, I like to take a photo or a still from a video and post it full screen on my story. This works really well when you post a carousel of multiple pictures, but some don't make the cut.

After you add in the photo, add a link to the story with either some short text or an emoji. The link should go to the post. The important thing is to keep people in the app. Instagram wants its users to stay on the platform so they can show more ads. I always add music to this kind of story as well.

Don't spam your audience with other people's content. This means don't post random memes and posts on your story. My rule of thumb is to only post someone else's content if you are in the photo or were tagged. For example, some people repost my content. When they do, I will post it on my story. If a friend posts a picture and tags me, I will also repost that. Every post should have a purpose.

Lead Magnets

I often get people DM-ing me on Twitter (now X) with their free lead magnet. I get fitness coaches who send me a 32-page paper on why I should be eating healthy. I get email copywriters sending me free lead magnets on how to write emails. I get user-generated content (UGC) creators sending me their UGC guides.

Guess what? It's not free. The price might be zero, but there is a cost. In this case, that cost is my time.

If you can't make your free stuff better than everyone else's paid stuff, people are never going to read your lead magnets.

Price is the monetary aspect of cost. Cost also includes the resources one must put in to achieve the desired result. Yes, there might not be any monetary cost, but there is a time cost, and my time is worth more than your crappy lead magnet.

There are five types of lead magnets: *educational, utility, entertainment, community based,* and *bottom of funnel.*

Educational Lead Magnets provide value through knowledge and expertise. They share your thoughts on things and educate people on a better way. This book, for example, is an educational lead magnet. The strategy here is to identify common questions or pain points your audience has trouble with and create content that addresses these issues.

For example, a YouTube video could be a lead magnet. If you're able to provide enough value, it will lead people to you.

The second type of lead magnet is a **Utility Lead Magnet**. Its purpose is to offer tools or resources that simplify a process for a user.

For example, if you have software that you use, you could "white label" (product or service produced by one company but rebranded and sold by another) it for free and use it as a lead magnet. Yes, this might cost you a little bit, but if you are selling a high-ticket item or service, you're going to be able to make that money back. This is why you must evaluate your cost to acquire a customer. If you know that number, you know how much you are able to spend on a lead magnet.

The goal of a utility lead magnet is to develop tools that save time or enhance productivity for your target audience. The more time you save, the less it costs.

Entertainment Lead Magnets are things like funny YouTube videos. The purpose is to engage and captivate the audience with enjoyable content they can easily consume. The strategy here is to create fun and interactive content that relates to your brand while entertaining your audience.

I would always throw an element of entertainment into any sort of lead magnet. For example, if you are making an educational video, make it entertaining as well. People will always respond well to entertainment. Look at Netflix. Although they don't really provide any value to the target audience, they're entertaining, and people will continue to pay every month. If you can entertain people, you can sell them as well.

Community-Based Lead Magnets foster a sense of belonging and connection among users. You can do this easily through a Facebook group, a Skool group, or any sort of group that you use. The strategy here is to offer exclusive access to communities where like-minded individuals can share ideas and experiences. People pay for connections.

If you can help people network with other individuals, they'll be much more likely to buy from you, and you will be perceived as an authority in the space.

The last kind of lead magnet is the **Bottom-of-Funnel Lead Magnet**. The purpose here is to convert people who are close to making a purchasing decision or warm leads into customers. The idea is to provide a tastier product or service that showcases its value and encourages a purchase. For example, you might give a free trial of a higher-ticket program instead of a lower-ticket program.

Sometimes, lead magnets can be paid as well. If you charge someone $17 for an ebook to collect an email, you are able to identify people who are going to be good prospects for your higher-ticket services.

The Lead Magnet Formula (M.A.G.N.E.T.I.C.)

Every lead magnet should have eight things:

1. Meaningful Value
2. Actionable Content
3. Goal Oriented
4. Niche Specific
5. Engaging Format
6. Timely and Relevant
7. Instant Value
8. Credibility Boost

The M stands for meaningful value. If your lead magnet lacks value or fails to offer practical solutions and insights or address the specific problems or needs of your target market, you'll struggle to get people to engage with it.

Value boils down to two things: time and money. The lead magnet should either save time or generate income. If it doesn't do either, it's simply not valuable enough. Typically, the correlation between the two is around $5 per minute. Saving someone one minute is equivalent to $5 worth of value.

Actionable content is key: providing clear steps and actions that users can take. For instance, I'm providing you with a step-by-step framework for your business here. It features easy-to-follow instructions and a clear outline, making it easy to extract actionable advice.

Goal-oriented lead magnets are those that align with business objectives, such as building an email list or establishing expertise.

Niche specificity is critical. Lead magnets should be tailored to your niche. Think about it: there's a much higher chance that someone will engage with me if I'm an authority in their industry. Speak their language and use terms they understand.

Lead magnets should also be engaging. If they're hard to consume, they will require too much effort and provide no value. Nowadays, people have the attention spans of goldfish. They won't be able to read through an entire document. Make the content as consumable as possible, like a video, a checklist, or a quick guide that can be downloaded and used promptly. If you're creating a book or graphic, ensure it's visually appealing and professionally designed to maintain interest.

All lead magnets should be timely and relevant, capitalizing on current trends or seasonal leads. Keep them regularly updated to remain pertinent.

Instant access is crucial. Time to first value is paramount in business. In the next chapter, we'll delve into client onboarding, but it's vital to deliver immediate value upon opt-in to satisfy customers' desire for instant gratification. This means making it easy to download or accessible online. For example, if you offer a free book and only charge for shipping, provide the first chapter online for free instantly. Remember, the longer someone takes to make a purchase decision, the more the perceived value diminishes.

Boost credibility with each lead magnet. Show testimonials or case studies to continue building trust. Showcase your expertise and authority in your field. If you are not seen as an industry expert, people won't trust you enough to read through the lead magnet. Remember, rapport is still necessary for lead magnets to work effectively.

CHAPTER 7

Backend Systems

When I got my first "real" job, it was at a local restaurant. This is when I first realized how important systems were. The restaurant ran smoothly because it had efficient systems in place for everything, from cleaning the floors to restocking supplies.

A few months later, another location was opening about 45 minutes away. For a while, their staff trained with us, and when the opening date finally rolled around, I went to the new store to help them train their team. The systems were different but still crucial to the role of the business.

This restaurant was a bit bigger than our store and had to serve more people on a daily basis. If there hadn't been a set way of doing things, nothing would have ever gotten done. To scale and grow, you need to have solid backend systems in place that can handle the increased workload while maintaining consistency and quality. The same principle applies to online businesses.

This experience taught me the value of adaptability and flexibility in systems. Not every business or situation is the same, so it's important to have a strong foundation, but improvements can always be made.

The backend serves as the foundation of any business and is the primary asset potential buyers seek. When acquiring a business, the focus is on its enterprise value. Systems and processes play a pivotal role in maximizing this value.

Business Operation Optimization Pyramid (BOOP)

During my time in business operations, I devised a straightforward framework you can easily implement in any business or even in your life. I realized that every recurring task can be categorized into three distinct areas: delegation, high ROI focus, and systemization. The pyramid is sorted based on the leverage of a task.

Delegation

First, you need to calculate your hourly rate. Below is a simple formula you can use. I don't believe in hourly pay, but I do believe in leverage. You can't tell if something is worth your time if you don't know what your time is worth.

Hourly Rate = (Yearly Profit Before Taxes)/2000

At the bottom of the pyramid are the tasks with the lowest leverage. These are things that are not worth your hourly rate and should be delegated or outsourced.

You can't scale with the mindset of "no one can do this better than I can." You are probably right, but you have to make sacrifices to scale. Remember to calculate the time it takes to find someone to do the work.

To effectively scale a business, you must delegate and outsource tasks that have low leverage. Working longer hours isn't always the solution. The key lies in maximizing what you do in the time you have. We only have 24 hours per day.

High ROI Focus

High ROI focus comes down to concentrating on the core business functions, like marketing, sales, and leadership. These change for each operator. For some, it may be delivery and hiring a marketing team. There are usually two to three core functions that you need to focus on. Leadership is always on the list.

As your business grows, your responsibilities in these areas evolve. In the early stages, you may handle all the sales calls, but as your company scales, you can delegate those calls to a sales team. This transition allows you to assume a leadership role in sales and focus on guiding your team to success.

Systemization

Systemization is the creation of standard operating procedures (SOPs) and streamlined processes. As you scale, you need to document the things you do on a daily basis so, when they are no longer worth your time, your company can continue to operate efficiently and effectively. Embracing systemization empowers you to optimize your operations and achieve your business goals with greater ease.

Funnel Mastery

One of the biggest turning points in my career was the discovery of funnels. Russell Brunson, CEO of ClickFunnels, wrote a book called *DotCom Secrets*. To this day, it is still one of my most referenced books.

When I first heard about a funnel, I thought of it just as a landing page. It took me a long time to define what it is, and even Russell Brunson says that he has issues defining it. I identify the funnel as a visual representation of the prospect's journey from cold lead to customer.

In other words, you're taking the prospect from not knowing who you are to becoming a buyer. A funnel has three simple steps: awareness, rapport, and sale.

Awareness

The first step is to make your prospect aware of what you do, who you are, and the problem you are solving. You should aim to capture maximum attention and channel it into the funnel right from the beginning. Awareness is a numbers game. The concern here is not so much qualifying but just getting the message out that you exist. As the prospect moves through awareness, they will discover more things about you.

Rapport

The next phase is establishing rapport. This entails using your free and paid lead magnets to convince individuals to engage with and explore the solutions you provide. Make sure you prioritize giving value before selling. Giving as much value as possible is the key to building rapport.

Micro-commitments are super important. The more you can get a customer to say yes to you, the more likely you will be to sell them. If you can get people to trust you, you can get them to buy from you. The easiest way to get people to trust you is by making them say yes to small things.

Another thing that can be added to the rapport stage is selling a cheaper, low-ticket product. People buy low-ticket products to learn more about you without having to drop a large amount of money on you. If you have a shitty low-ticket product, people are never going to buy your high-ticket product because they're not going to trust you, but if your low-ticket product is filled with golden nuggets, they're a lot more likely to buy your high-ticket product in the future.

This phase is also a spot to filter out bad prospects. If someone isn't willing to spend $37 with you, it is highly unlikely they will be willing to spend thousands of dollars on a high-ticket product.

Sale

The final step in the process is getting paid and sealing the deal. The approach may vary based on the company's size, either more hands-on or hands-off. For instance, if you're offering a $7 lead magnet, it may not be necessary to engage in a call. However, for higher-priced programs, a call is likely required to build extra rapport before the transaction.

Draw Your Funnels

Crafting a customer touchpoint map is incredibly important when outlining your funnels. I like to use a flowchart or a whiteboard to sketch out every step of the journey my customers will embark on, from initial contact to becoming a loyal patron.

Choosing a funnel with a landing page is much better than a regular website. Its only job is to help people move to the next part of the funnel.

Recently, I decided to get rid of all my websites and transition solely to funnels. Of course, I maintain a basic homepage, but its objective is to seamlessly direct visitors to the appropriate funnel based on their specific needs and interests.

The next step is the opt-in page, where you'll collect email addresses or phone numbers. Some funnels include upsells, depending on what's being offered. After that is the order page, where people actually make purchases. Finally, there's the thank-you page, where customers receive their product and access their purchase.

CRM Systems

When I first started working with my mom in her accounting business, I discovered one big bottleneck: the spider web of CRMs (Customer relationship management systems).

I've seen it time and time again. Business owners don't even know where their customers are because they use six different CRMs. They use ten different software products and can't keep up with everything.

When I am looking for a CRM, I want an all-in-one solution. Currently, GoHighLevel is my go-to because it has everything all in one place. Whichever platform you use, make sure it has useful core features such as a comprehensive database of all customer contact details, including name, email, phone number, social media profiles, etc. This basic information will allow you to reach out and communicate with your prospects and customers.

You should also be able to keep a communication history, a detailed record of every interaction between your business and the customer. Past interactions will provide more context about the customer, helping you give them a better experience in the future.

You should also be able to track customer behavior, such as purchase history, product or service usage, website usage, etc. This data can provide insights into customer preferences and habits, which helps you make a more personalized marketing and service delivery approach.

The biggest thing is that you have the ability to collect data. You don't want to guess.

Pipelines

Your goal when selling is to move people through a pipeline. A pipeline is similar to a Kanban board, like Trello, where you can track the status of your clients through each part of your funnel. In my high-ticket pipeline, I have seven columns in which I can move people depending on the stage of the funnel they are in.

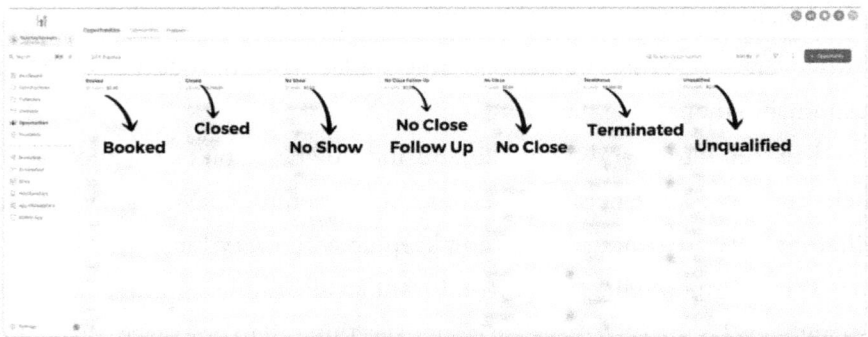

- **Booked** – When the client has booked a call.
- **Closed** – The client closed AND paid.
- **No show** – The client didn't show up for the scheduled call.

- **No Close Follow Up** – The client didn't close on the first call and needs to be nurtured through automation.
- **No close** – The client didn't close or got disqualified on the call.
- **Terminated** – The client paid but is no longer a client.
- **Unqualified** – The client was disqualified through the pre-call workflow.

These metrics help me monitor various parts of my systems and establish targeted data to make logical decisions. If you ain't tracking, you're slacking.

If you have a multi-stage client process, like onboarding, you can track it in a pipeline by breaking down the process into distinct stages. Each stage represents a step in the client journey. You can use a CRM tool to visualize this pipeline, allowing you to move clients through stages as they progress, add notes, and track key metrics to ensure a smooth onboarding experience. This method provides clear visibility into where each client is in the process and what actions are needed to advance them to the next stage.

The Team Pipeline

One extremely important thing that most people don't talk about is the talent pipeline. Whoever has the bigger pool of talent will be able to hire more qualified people and build a stronger team.

I believe that it is crucial to constantly be on the lookout for top talent and actively engage with potential candidates even if you don't currently have a role for them. At one point, I lost an editor while I was traveling. I had three videos due the next day for clients, and the editing hadn't even started on them. Without a pool of editors to choose from, I wouldn't have been able to replace the one I lost so quickly. I had a new person filling the role and working on the videos within two hours of the old editor telling me that he was resigning.

You should treat your team just like your customers. They were on a journey before joining your company, just as a customer. I will go more in depth on this in the chapter on hiring.

We go through a few different pipeline stages: applied, for when someone has filled out an application form; disqualified, which happens automatically for some fields and manually for others; qualified sent booking, meaning that I qualified them and sent them a booking link; and call booked, which means that they booked their interview call. There's also a hired section, a fired section, and a waitlist column for people who have been qualified but are not needed at the moment. Whenever people book a call, they are automatically placed in my pipeline in the booked stage.

Onboarding Systems

Onboarding systems are the welcome mat to the castle of customer retention and are some of the most important things customers look at. Time to first value (TTFV) is crucial in a service-based business. Sixty-three percent of customers think onboarding is the key to deciding to subscribe to a product, and 74% of potential customers will switch to another solution if the onboarding process is complicated. (Source: Userpilot)

The Welcome Mat Framework

You should think of your onboarding systems like a funnel. You need to move prospects through a series of steps that will educate them on your service and explain the value they'll receive to further reinforce their decision to pay you.

Regret-free purchases are all about instant action.

Every idle minute after purchase is a minute of buyer's remorse.

My onboarding funnel is built out as a course inside of GoHighLevel (a comprehensive marketing platform, encompassing customer relationship management features). Step one is to receive the payment. Whenever a client pays, they automatically get moved into the closed position. After that, the team and I get a Slack notification that tells us they were moved through the pipeline.

Then the new client gets an onboarding email delivered to their inbox, with access to their Google Drive folders, which are automatically created through Zapier, and a link to access the onboarding form. Whenever this form is completed, I get another notification in Slack that says so.

Their responses also get added to a Google Doc that gets sent to the prospect and the team so we can access it later on and measure the progress from where a client was when they started.

Second, I have the client record a quick 10- to 15-minute video about their story and how they got into the industry. This is one of the few client tasks that they must do. This is so I can learn about them while also training up the teams for their business.

Next, the client shares account access with me to all the software I need. I must have a layout of what accounts they actually have to share so it's clear in the future.

The next step is to book their kickoff call where we discuss a few different things about their business and get them ready to go. If you're selling anything high ticket, this is a must.

There are also a few manual tasks. I try to automate as much as possible, but sometimes, it's just not possible or smart to automate. For one thing, the course is added to their client database.

I also created a new CRM Snapshot (a clone of a GoHighLevel account that can be imported into another account with all the same systems) for them because we manage the CRM and provide it at the cost of our services. This is just something that I offer in my business that I have to do manually. You probably have other tasks.

I'll also create a custom Slack channel for each of my clients. There are a few different manual tasks, but I try to automate as much as possible. You can also outsource the tasks as you grow.

Automation

I could get more in depth here, but I'm not going to because the automated tasks change all the time. What I will say is that automation is one of the most crucial parts of any business.

Payroll is typically the biggest expense for a business. Yes, it's great to create jobs, but you also have to keep your business afloat, and the only way to do that is to optimize the amount of profit you are making per time unit spent by you or your team.

If you can't make any profit, you're not going to be creating jobs. Instead, you're going to be getting rid of the jobs you already have because your company's going to go bankrupt.

If you create too many overpaying jobs too quickly, the business will collapse, leading to no jobs at all.

The rise in the cost of employees is making A-players win even more than they already were. It is better to have a small team of A-players than a large team of mindless workers.

You need to embrace automation. It's not going to replace you, but the people who automate will replace the ones who don't.

Automation saves you time and money and can also help with the scalability and growth of your company. When you sell a company, the biggest things you're selling are your systems and processes.

If you don't have automation in place and have a manual task, it's going to lower the enterprise value of your company.

There are a lot of different tools to help you automate, and the landscape is constantly changing, but Zapier is one of the top players at the moment. I also like using Make (formerly Integromat) and my CRM, GoHighLevel.

If your CRM doesn't have built-in automation capabilities, you need to switch. ClickFunnels and GoHighLevel both have these.

If you don't know how to automate, you can bring in an automation expert. You can hire these people using the techniques I'm going to teach you in the Building an Army section of this book. They can help you solve repetitive tasks and problems.

Action Item: Write down all the tasks that you have done in your business for two weeks straight. I want you to map out every single thing you do in your calendar with as much detail as possible. This list should be as long as you can make it. Then, sit down for one to two hours at the end of the two weeks and figure out what you can automate. Repeat this process and continue to automate more. This one to two hours might cost a little time, but it will save you hundreds of hours in the long term.

CHAPTER 8

Sales

In a world that moves at an unprecedented pace, where technological advancements shape and reshape industries overnight, one skill remains timeless: sales. It is this enduring art of persuasion and influence that is the lifeblood of any thriving economy. Without it, the most innovative products would remain undiscovered, valuable services unnoticed, and groundbreaking ideas left untouched in the minds of their creators.

Sales is an essential craft because it transcends transactions. Sales is the art of building relationships, understanding human behavior, and cultivating trust. These skills aren't confined to selling a product or service; they permeate every aspect of our lives. From convincing a girl to love you to negotiating with your child about bedtime hours—sales is the key.

The significance of sales isn't confined to personal gain. It possesses a transformative power that can change the world. Think about impactful movements, such as civil rights or climate change—all were sold to us through powerful narratives and persuasive leaders who knew how to sell their cause effectively.

I always say **marketing, sales,** and **leadership** are the three highest-leverage skills. And from the start, you should be selling. Sales will be one of the last things to be automated and replaced by AI because people love human connection.

Sales Mindset

In an online service-based business, the right mindset is your most valuable asset—it's paramount to success. This mindset, which we call "the Sales Mindset," is built out of belief, conviction, and unity with your prospects. It's the lifeblood that empowers you to influence others and create beneficial exchanges for both parties involved.

Belief in your product or service is the cornerstone of this mindset. If you genuinely believe in what you're selling, selling isn't manipulative. It becomes a moral duty. For example, if you sell fitness products, you know that your product changes lives. You have an obligation to sell your product.

You have knowledge of a product or service that can alleviate pain points, solve problems, and enrich lives. By not persuading your prospects to buy into it, you are doing them a disservice—holding back sauce that could potentially bring significant value to their lives.

My rule of thumb in sales is to make sure that whatever I'm selling is either solving a pain or giving the customer gain. If your product is not doing at least one of those things, you should find something else to sell—not just because of how hard it is to sell but also the ethical implications of selling something that isn't benefiting the prospect.

Belief alone, however powerful it may be, won't suffice—you need to achieve unity with your prospects as well. Unity implies understanding their needs profoundly and empathizing with their situation.

Every prospect you engage with should feel understood and valued—not just seen as another notch on the sales ladder. This unity creates trust, a fundamental ingredient in any successful sales relationship.

So, how do we cultivate this unity? Start by listening more than you speak. Understand the prospect's pain points, aspirations, and fears before offering anything. Use open-ended questions that encourage them to share more about their needs and wants. Treat them as if they are your best friend.

Always deliver value first before asking for anything in return. This could be through free content like blogs, webinars, or even complimentary consultations where the prospect experiences firsthand the quality of your service without any financial commitment.

Give them sauce and treat them like a boss.

Sales, at its core, is a fascinating numbers game. It's a journey where every interaction with a prospect holds the potential to bring you closer to closing a deal.

The more prospects you can provide the highest level of service to, the better your sales numbers will be.

Sales Calls

Sales calls are crucial for service-based businesses to acquire new clients and grow their customer base. I still have the notes from my very first sales call. I hopped on the call and thought it was going really well, but there was no structure at all. When I got to the end, instead of having any prepared questions, I just said, "Would this be something you're interested in?" The guy obviously said no because I did not have any sort of structure.

I want to save you all the time that it took me to learn this skill. At the end of the day, we want money, so let's explore a structured approach that will help you conduct effective sales calls.

Pre-Call Flow

Before making a sales call, preparation is key. You need to know your prospect as if they are your best friend so you can build rapport. Before your calls, you should qualify the prospect and make sure they are a good fit, so you're not wasting time. All this info should be in the CRM, so you should at least glance at it before the call starts.

I usually spend about five to 10 minutes researching the prospect so I know where we have room to build rapport. I check out their social media pages and any other info I can find on them. I also review all the messages I've sent them inside of the CRM.

Next, I focus on getting my energy right. No one wants someone who's about to fall asleep to hop on a sales call with them. People need to be put into a buying state. People want a reason to buy, but you have to give them one. If you are lazy and not boosting their mood, they are not going to buy from you.

You might say I'm crazy, but every top salesman I've ever met does some sort of exercise before the call. For me, that is taking a set of push-ups to a rate of perceived exertion (RPE) of seven (three reps from failure).

The other thing I do is play some high-dopamine-releasing music. I need something to get me in the state of winning. For me, that is David Goggins SoundCloud remixes. Most people consider Goggins to be "The Toughest Man Alive." He is a retired Navy SEAL and the only member of the U.S. Armed Forces to complete SEAL training, Army Ranger School, and Air Force Tactical Air Controller training. He also has run multiple 100+ mile races—his story and his message really hit home for me. For you, it could be anything. I want something a little bit more hardcore so my dopamine receptors fire in my brain.

Just as you don't want to buy from someone who is asleep, you don't want to buy from someone who is on their phone the entire time. Power it off and put it away. If anything urgent comes up, you can get texts on your Mac. And if you're running on PC, too bad, so sad. Turn your phone off. You need to be present in the moment.

The last thing I do before I jump into the call is pray. I pray for all the good things that God has done and show my gratitude. I also pray that the call goes well and I'm able to serve the person at the highest level and help them with whatever they need.

Discovery

The discovery phase is where you gather information about your prospect's needs, challenges, and goals. We are gathering ammunition to use in the close.

The discovery phase is the initial stage of any sales process, where the sales representative delves deep into the prospect's world to find out what drives them, their pain points, and their vision for a future free from these challenges. This phase is pivotal to creating a strong foundation for a successful sales relationship and closing the deal. The goal is to foster strong relationships with your prospects so you can offer solutions that truly resonate with their needs. The discovery phase is broken into five parts, listed below.

1. Introduction and Context Setting:

Start the call by introducing yourself and setting the context for the call. Explain the purpose of the call and reassure them that this is a chance to dig deep into their needs and challenges.

You should always be on calls before the prospect. Yes, you may have to show up several minutes early. That's ok. You need to be the first person to speak. I usually start by asking if they can hear me.

You also need to give an overview of how the call will run. This will help to assert a frame and build you as an authority. The prospect needs to perceive you as a powerful figure to buy, but they also need to see that you are on their level. Don't get cocky but make sure they know that you already have a plan for how this call is going to go. Usually, I say something along the lines of "I'll ask you some questions, and if I feel like you might benefit from the program, I'll walk you through our process and how we can help you. Sounds fair enough?"

2. Understanding the Prospect's Motivation:

Find out why they're interested in your services. This will give you a better understanding of their expectations and goals and let you know if you can actually help them. I like to clarify their intentions early on and ask them why they booked the call in the first place. Here, we are not looking for a shallow answer. We are looking for our first micro-commitment. We want to ask them something along the lines of "What attracted you to book a call with us?" or "What are you hoping to get out of this call?"

3. Current State:

To gain a better understanding of the prospect's current situation, it is important to obtain a clear picture. Sales is like Google Maps; before you can get to the place you want to go, you have to analyze where you are currently at. If you don't know the current pains, you don't know what problems you have to fix.

You need the prospect to open up and share their current challenges or pain points. This will help you determine if your product or service is a good fit for them and how you can provide a solution to their problems. As sales professionals, we must be active listeners and empathize with the prospect's struggles. Ask open-ended questions such as "What are the biggest challenges you're facing right now?" or "What keeps you up at night in terms of your business?"

We want to make our product the bridge between their current state and their desired state.

Current State   **Desired State**

4. Goal Identification:

Once you have a clear understanding of the prospect's current situation, it is important to establish their goals and desired outcomes. If you don't know where you want to go, how will Google Maps get you there? Understanding the prospect's goals will help you tailor your solution and offer to their specific needs. This also helps build trust with the prospect, as they can see that you are invested in their success.

This is where it is crucial to escape commission breath. Your goal is to change their life so they can go from their current state to their desired state. Typically, these questions consist of two types of goals: short-term and long-term. I ask where they see themselves in six months to a year, but I also ask where they see themselves ten years down the road. If they have a hard time identifying a long-term goal, encourage them to think about their ultimate vision and how this business can help them get there.

I then ask about the impacts this goal will have, how reaching it will benefit their family or what it will mean for their life on a day-to-day basis. This is called selling the vacation.

To recap, you need to determine their short-term goals (six months to a year), their long-term goals (vision/mission), and how your business can help them achieve these goals.

5. Problem-Solving and Commitment:

The objective is to understand the impact of the pain they are experiencing on their lives and guide them toward recognizing our product as the solution to their problems. It's important to note that the aim is not simply to persuade them but rather to empower them to embrace the solution as their own. Recognizing that people have a natural inclination to resist being told what to do, we can overcome this hurdle by presenting the solution in a way that makes it their own idea.

If they think that the solution you're offering can actually help them, they're a lot more likely to buy it. This is the spot in the call where you should bring up testimonials and case studies of people who have had similar experiences. This will instill belief in the prospect that they can get similar results.

Action Item: Write down all the problems, solutions, and the states in which the problems are solved. You need to instill belief in yourself (and your sales team) that your product does what you say it does.

Presentation and Value Proposition

After realizing we can assist them, we smoothly transition into the presentation. Our goal is to showcase our solution as a groundbreaking opportunity that can solve their problems.

We're not just selling a product or a service; we're selling a vision. This is where you showcase your solution and the value it brings to the customer. They need to see the potential of what they could achieve by choosing you. Here are the five steps of the presentation:

Methodology

The methodology is a framework that you share with the prospect. For example, when I was first getting into the world of appointment setting, my framework was called Organic Engagement Amplification Retargeting. It's a bit of a mouthful, I know.

The point is, because I shared my methodology with prospects, they were able to understand how I approach appointment setting and how my approach differs from others. It also gave them a sense of structure and confidence in our process.

How the Product/Service Gets Rid of Pain

The main focus of our methodology is to alleviate the prospect's challenges. By linking each feature of our solution to a specific problem they're facing, we show them how our product/service can remove these issues. This isn't just about selling features; it's about providing solutions.

What There Is to Gain

Our solution is designed not only to address immediate concerns but also to provide long-term relief from recurring problems. We delve into how our solution can help improve their business processes, reduce inefficiencies, and eliminate the root causes of their pain points.

The Difference

We differentiate ourselves by showcasing what makes our solution unique. We highlight the unique aspects of our product/service that set it apart from those of competitors, ensuring the prospect understands why choosing us is the best decision for their business.

Similar Result

To reinforce our claims, we share testimonials from satisfied customers who have faced similar challenges. These success stories serve as proof of our solution's effectiveness and demonstrate its potential to deliver the same positive results for the prospect.

Price

To maximize the impact and effectiveness of your strategy, you must refrain from revealing the price too early. If you have done your job correctly, you should have already sold the product on the front end, and the only issue should be with the price. It is much harder to overcome objections when a prospect says that the product is not what they are looking for or is not valuable enough to them. Your only objection should be the price. That's why we leave it for last.

Price is only an issue when the perceived value of the product or service is less than the money required to obtain it. It's important to allow the prospect to see the potential return on investment and understand why your product or service is worth the price.

If they ask for the price too early, tell them that you need to know more about their situation before you can give them a price because you do custom plans and want to make sure that you're giving them the best service for them specifically. This will make them feel special and more likely to buy.

After the presentation, we are not going to tell them the price instantly. We are going to ask if they have any other questions *about the program specifically.* If they have any questions about value, you can go ahead and address those objections from the beginning. If they say no, ask them if they have any questions in general. Nine times out of 10, they will ask for the price here.

I implement a trial close before I even unveil the price. I ask them, "Is this something that you're ready to be a part of today?" Three things could happen. Sometimes, they will say yes, and that is when you unveil the price. If this happens, we need to assume the close. I will say something along the lines of "Awesome. So, the next step to get you onboarded is to get that payment sent over. The price is [XYZ]. What would be the best email to send the payment link to?" Don't ask them if that is okay. They will tell you if it's not. Assume the close.

Sometimes, they will give you an objection about why they don't know if the program is right for them. You can try to overcome this, but make sure you are being ethical and the program can actually provide some benefit.

Sometimes, prospects will ask the price here, and that's where we transition into part three of the call.

When you present the price, the way you act changes the prospect's perception. If you act like the price is a ton of money and not worth it, the prospect will not buy. Remember, you are their friend. If you have your customers' best interests at heart, you are doing them a favor. Be confident when presenting the price.

After you present the price, you will *not* speak a word until your prospect responds. The first person to talk loses the sale. Yes, it will be awkward. I have sat in silence on calls for 30 seconds before. Do not break. Do not justify your price unless you are asked to. You have already justified it in the presentation.

Close and Objection Handling

There are a ton of small tricks that you can use to increase your close rate, but the one I use the most is called the assumed close. You have to have a delusional belief that the prospect is going to buy every time. You are actually serving and helping your customers by doing so.

I don't ask my prospects if they are ready to move forward. Instead, I change the way I word things. For example, I ask them if they are ready to change their life, not if they are ready to buy the program. Remember, they don't care about the methodology or the product. The only thing they care about is results.

I'm also not going to ask them if they are ready to move forward. I am going to ask them questions that make it easy to say "yes" and hard to say "no."

I have two closing statements.

1. "What would be the best email to send the payment link to?"
2. "If I can get you [XYZ] result, would that offend you in any way?"

If people have concerns, they will bring them up. Don't assume they have concerns. Instead, focus on presenting the benefits of your product or service and how it can help improve their life. Use empowering language to make them feel like they are making a positive change for themselves.

Objections

When overcoming objections, don't use pushy sales tactics or try to force customers into a decision. Instead, listen to their needs and concerns and address them in a genuine and empathetic manner. Show them that you truly care about helping them achieve their goals and improve their life.

Having a strategic approach to objections is crucial for success. As the saying goes, "Failing to plan is planning to fail." If you prepare enough, you can overcome every objection. By anticipating and preparing for all possible objections, you can position yourself to overcome any challenge that comes your way. The way to stay confident in your objection handling is to memorize the lines you are going to say for every objection. To create an effective objection plan, start by identifying your top 10 to 20 objections and develop word tracks for each one. Dedicate 30 to 60 minutes a day to practicing these objection-handling techniques. Remember, this is an integral aspect of your business. If you have a sales team, make them practice together daily as well.

All objections come down to one of three problems: lack of scarcity/urgency, lack of trust/credibility, or insufficient value for the price. The following are the top objections I get in my business, followed by some tips for addressing each of them.

Scarcity/Urgency	Trust/Credibility	Price/Value/Cost
• I need to think about it. • I need to talk to my wife. • I'm not ready to make a decision yet. • I'm just looking.	• I'm not sure if it will help me reach my goals. • I've been burned in the past. • Do you have any testimonials/case studies?	• The price is too high. • I don't want to buy without _____. • What's your best price?

Scarcity/Urgency

These objections often arise due to a lack of perceived value or urgency. Often, they are smoke screens for the real problem: price. If a customer doesn't feel that they need your product or service urgently, or if they don't see its unique value, they may want to "think about it" or consult with others before making a decision.

To overcome this, it's important to build value in your product or service so that the prospect sees it as a worthwhile investment despite the perceived pressure. Add more scarcity and urgency to the sale. You can do this by highlighting limited quantities, making special offers, or providing time-sensitive discounts.

Trust/Credibility

Trust and credibility are crucial in any business transaction. If customers have been burned in the past, they may hesitate before trusting another company. They may question whether your product or service will truly help them reach their goals. The reason for this, 99% of the time, is that you failed to build up enough rapport in the discovery process. To address these objections, businesses frequently offer testimonials or case studies as evidence of their credibility and effectiveness.

Be transparent and honest about your products/services and their benefits. Address any negative reviews or feedback openly and show how you've improved since then. Building a relationship over time can also help establish trust.

Price/Value/Cost

The objection "I can't afford it" is quite common and usually indicates that the value of your offering hasn't been effectively demonstrated. It could mean that your product lacks value or you haven't effectively conveyed its worth. In most cases, it's the latter. It's crucial to avoid commoditization, as it leads to both scenarios. If customers perceive the price as too high, it means they don't see enough value in what you're offering. They may want something extra ("I don't want to buy without _____") to justify the cost or try to negotiate ("What's your best price?") to feel they're getting a good deal. The problem here is that you didn't build enough perceived value in the sale.

Key Sales Techniques

There are many small techniques and strategies that you need to adopt to close more deals. Here are my top five:

Scripts and Systems

Having a well-defined system and structure in place is crucial for scalability. Sales systems provide a structured approach to the sales process, ensuring consistency and efficiency. They act as a roadmap, guiding sales professionals through each stage of the customer journey. Without a well-designed system in place, scaling your sales efforts becomes an uphill battle. A lack of systems hinders growth and limits your ability to replicate success.

While scripts can serve as a useful starting point, relying solely on word-for-word scripts can hinder genuine connection and adaptability. People want human connection. Customers value authentic conversations, and rigid scripts can make interactions feel robotic and impersonal. Every customer is unique, and a one-size-fits-all approach will not resonate with their specific needs and preferences.

Having a structured approach to sales provides a framework that keeps sales professionals on track and focused. It allows for flexibility and adaptability while maintaining a consistent flow and message. By following a structure, sales professionals can confidently navigate conversations, address customer pain points, and guide prospects toward making informed decisions.

I already laid out my entire system above, so take it and build a system of your own.

Problem Retargeting

Problem retargeting is a unique approach I developed that revolves around refocusing customers' attention on their actual needs and demonstrating how your product or service can address them. Instead of simply telling them their pain points, the key is to guide them to realize these pain points on their own. By asking thought-provoking questions multiple times, you can bring out these pain points effectively.

For instance, I would often ask fitness coaches, "Why are you special, different, or the one?" Typically, their initial response was something generic, such as their personality or accountability, which everyone else also offers. This is when they would start to realize the difficulty in coming up with a compelling answer. At this point, I would re-target the same problem by asking, "What would make someone choose you over the competition?" More often than not, they would struggle to provide a satisfactory answer.

The key is to repeat these questions, gradually leading them toward a breaking point where they recognize their pain points. Throughout a sales call, the aim is to create as many of these breakthrough moments as possible. By doing so, you can effectively highlight the value your product or service brings and drive conversions.

Anchoring

Anchoring is a psychological tactic used in negotiations where a reference point or anchor is established. Here, it involves setting a specific point or figure, commonly known as the anchor, in a sales discussion. The purpose is to create a perception that the product is inexpensive by initially presenting a high reference price.

For instance, when a car salesman mentions a price at the beginning of a negotiation, it sets the tone for the rest of the conversation and becomes the anchor. If subsequent discussions lead to a lower price, the customer's perception of value and fairness is often influenced by that original anchor price. Consider this scenario: if I were to convey that my product has a value worth $36,000 but I would charge only $3,600, it might be perceived as inexpensive even if it is not. On the other hand, if I simply state that the product costs $3,600, it may be perceived as expensive.

Labeling

Labeling is a highly effective technique for fostering rapport and comprehension with prospects. It involves attributing specific qualities to prospects, whether they align or differ. For instance, if a prospect raises a price objection, one might respond by suggesting that they value quality over affordability, thereby encouraging them to reconsider their objection. This practice enhances communication and strengthens relationships with potential clients.

Negative Labels

Employing negative labels is a technique that gets strong reactions from customers. Negative labels involve making untrue statements. For instance, you could ask if someone likes to purchase cheap items. This approach compels prospects to acknowledge their preference for quality, making it easier to guide the conversation.

Mirroring

Mirroring involves repeating a prospect's words at the end of a sentence. There are two types of mirroring: matching energy and matching words. You need both. Let me provide you with a sample conversation to illustrate this technique.

Prospect: I've been trying to get into shape, but it's been tough doing it alone.

Coach: Tough doing it alone? (Mirroring)

Prospect: Yes. I have wanted to do it for a long time, but I have no one to hold me accountable. I have tried losing weight before, but I haven't found much success. I feel like I have tried everything.

Coach:	You feel like you have tried everything? (Mirroring)
Prospect:	Yes. I have tried keto, vegan, carnivore, and Mediterranean diets in the past but haven't found any success. I want to get results fast.
Coach:	I completely understand. (Justifying Their Failures). You seem like the type of person who wants long-term results and not just a quick fix to the problem. Am I right? (Labeling)
Prospect:	Yes. I want to be healthy for a long time so I can be around longer for my family.
Coach:	So, you want to live longer to have more time with your family? (Labeling)
Prospect:	Yes. My family is a huge priority, but I don't know if I can support them well with where I am currently at.
Coach:	You don't know if you can support them with where you are at? (Mirroring)

Certainty

To gain a prospect's confidence, you must consider four crucial factors: relevance, reputation, results, and rapport. First and foremost, your product must be relevant to the prospect's specific needs. Next, you need to establish a solid reputation as the go-to expert in your field. Prospects need to be convinced that your company can deliver the desired outcomes, increasing their chances of success. Lastly, you need to build rapport. Prospects must trust you, your product, and your company wholeheartedly.

Certainty cannot be transferred if you lack confidence in what you offer. You must have the delusional belief that your product is the best.

As Jordan Belfort, the "Wolf of Wall Street," often emphasizes, first impressions are crucial. Within seconds, hiring managers and sales professionals can assess a person's suitability.

Therefore, it is important to project sharpness and expertise from the outset. Embrace judgment and leverage it to your advantage. Strive to be judged positively, as this will alleviate many of your challenges.

CHAPTER 9

Building an Army

Growing up, we were all told in school that there are two ways to increase the amount of money you have:

1.   **Make more money.**
2.   **Cut expenses.**

While this is mathematically true, cutting costs is typically what kills most business owners. Yes, you should get rid of pointless costs, but that won't make a significant difference to the bottom line.

One of the biggest lessons I have learned from my successful business friends is that winners don't focus on cutting monetary expenses; they focus on cutting time expenses so they can make more money.

Yes, you need to minimize expenses and increase profit, but you can cut your costs all the way down to bankruptcy.

Instead of cutting, try building an army of soldiers ready to go to war on your behalf.

Some people think scaling businesses is about doing more things to make more money, and some think it is about doing less and outsourcing it all. Both people are wrong. Scaling companies is about leverage and increasing your hourly rate.

How do you do this? You buy your time by hiring people. I call this method "Growth Hacking."

Your team's the backbone of your business, and you shouldn't be doing everything yourself. You don't have time to learn all of the skills you will need. If you hire 10 people with 10 years of experience each, that is a hundred total years of combined experience.

Businesses have two primary acquisition functions: the acquisition of clients and the acquisition of talent. You should think of hiring as a second type of acquisition. Everything flows and moves the same way.

You should use the same funnel system that we talked about in the acquisition unit to build out a continuous flow of potential talent leads and maintain a strong pipeline. The flow of team leads is just as important as the flow of prospective client leads.

A-Players

I have a five-step process for identifying and hiring A-players.

Applicants typically begin by filling out an application form on my website, often discovering it through platforms like Indeed and OnlineJobs.ph if I am hiring from the Philippines.

Afterward, they proceed to an interview, where we evaluate their competence, commitment, enthusiasm for the role, and what they can bring to our team.

Sixty-eight percent of candidates believe that a company's treatment during the hiring process reflects how it treats its employees (Source: CareerBuilder). Similar to a traditional client funnel, having a streamlined onboarding process is crucial. Talent onboarding ensures that new hires gain a comprehensive understanding of business culture, required skills, and expectations.

Employee retention is of utmost importance in business. The cost of losing a team member varies based on their role level. As a rule of thumb, we calculate the loss as 50% of salary for entry-level workers, 150% for mid-level employees, and 250% for high-level positions. For instance, losing someone with a $100,000 salary would amount to a loss of approximately $250,000. Yikes.

The Tri-Harmony Talent Matrix

The Tri-Harmony Talent Matrix refers to the three general areas on which I evaluate potential team members: **Cultural Consonance, Confidence Compatibility,** and **Commitment Congruence.** Under these categories are the specific traits I am looking for in those looking to join our team.

Cultural Consonance:

The extent to which individuals align with their society's norms, values, and behaviors, impacting their mental and physical health.

- **Value Alignment**
  The first thing I always look for is if the candidate's values align with ours. Do they have personal ethics that resonate with the core values of the company? It's very important to lay out the core values and show the candidate what they need to know.

- **Team Dynamics**
  Will the individual boost team morale or drag it down? There is no neutral. What will the prospective team member do to boost morale, and how does their energy add to the team?

- **Optimal Environment**
  Can they thrive in the company-specific work atmosphere and culture? One thing to look at, if it's a work-from-home role, is that they're actually disciplined enough to get their work done and not lie about their hours.

Competence Compatibility

- **Proven Prowess**

  Does the candidate bring a track record of success that is relevant to the team? What results have they gotten in the past?

- **Skill Spectrum**

  Are the candidate's abilities and skills in sync with the technical and soft skills required for the role? Do they actually have the skills needed to help you grow the business, or are they coming in brand new? Never hire on potential; always hire on experience.

Commitment Congruence

- **Role Enthusiasm**

  Does the candidate exhibit genuine excitement and passion for the responsibilities of the role? Are they excited to come to work on a daily basis, or are they acting like they're tired and complaining about work behind your back? If you can't see how their energy will positively impact the team, they're not a good hire.

- **Growth Oriented**

  Are they motivated by the prospect of personal and professional development within the role? Sometimes, you get a job to learn instead of to earn. It's not always about what they're going to make, especially with a small business. They might not make as much, but are they excited to come to work? And where do they see themselves in 10 years? What are their goals?

- **Vision Fit**

  The vision of the person needs to fit inside the company's vision. If it doesn't, they won't be there for the long term.

The Perfect Application Form

Now, we're going to apply the tri-harmony talent matrix to our perfect application form.

Before we ask any of those questions, we want to ask some general competency questions. These are going to be three to five checkbox questions that will automatically disqualify the prospect if they answer no to any of them.

These are things like: **Are you coachable? Are you here for the long term? Are you a hard worker?** If they don't check these boxes, they are automatically disqualified from the system to save some time.

Ninety-eight percent of people will hit yes on these questions, even if they're not. However, the people who hit no are definitely not people you want on your team. So, the questions add an extra layer of security for you or your hiring manager.

Cultural Consonance

- **Value alignment**

  "How do you embody our core values?" List the core values. Often, people will try to write a long response using AI. If this is the case, instantly disqualify them. What you're looking for here is an honest list of the person's core values so you can see if they actually align with yours. You want a paragraph, not just a sentence, and not an essay.

- **Team dynamics**

  "What can you bring to the team?" Intrapreneurs will give a great explanation of how they're going to be a leader inside of the team. Here, we're looking for soft skills and the value they feel they can add to the team.

- **Optimal Environment**

  "Describe your optimal work environment and what you would do on a day-to-day basis." Here, we're trying to figure out if they like remote or office work. This is where you're going to find out the energy they have and what they're going to bring to the team. You also want to get an idea of their daily routine and workflow.

Competence Compatibility

- **Proven Prowess**

  "What do you currently do for work?" Look and see what they're currently doing right now and what experience they have. Remember, the best of the best are already working for a company. If they say they are unemployed, it doesn't always mean they should be instantly disqualified, but sometimes, it can be a leading indicator.

- **Skill Spectrum**

  "What are your greatest skills as they relate to the job?" You want them to provide you with what they have knowledge about. The goal here is to find a puzzle piece that fills a lacking part of your business. For example, if you suck at sales, hiring a salesman with proven sales experience might be a good choice.

  "Do you have any previous experience doing [XYZ]? Explain." If you're in sales, for example, you would ask the candidate what their lifetime sales volume was.

Commitment Congruence

- **Role Enthusiasm**

  "Why did this role specifically excite you?" Here, we're looking to see what genuine excitement they have about helping others and winning in their life.

- **Growth Orientation + Vision Fit**

  "What is your vision for your life?" Here you want to analyze their vision and how it fits inside of yours. If your vision is to make a million dollars in revenue and their goal is to make three million dollars in profit for themselves, they're probably not going to be a good fit. Their vision has to fit inside of yours.

- **Loom Video**

  "Create a Loom video that explains why we should choose you." A player will go above and beyond to get whatever result they need. If they don't have their camera on, disqualify them. If they use an old video that is prerecorded, disqualify them. If they don't seem like a good fit, disqualify them. The Loom video is to test their commitment level. In the video, we're looking for three things: body language, speaking patterns, and content.

  Body language: What is their physical stature? Are they sitting up or slouching? Do they appear confident on camera? If you're hiring someone in the sales space, they must build rapport with you through the video. If there's no rapport, they're probably not going to be a good fit for a sales role.

  Speaking patterns: Do they use a lot of filler words, or are they very clear and concise in what they say? Are they confident? Do they mess up their words a lot? What's their mood? Are they hyped up and pumped, or are they lazy and unenthusiastic?

  Content: Is what they are saying relevant? If they're just talking nonsense and aren't using the language associated with that role, they're probably not a good fit.

Conducting Interviews

- **Introduction**

  During the introduction of your interview, you need to maintain a frame. To do this, you have to be the first person to talk. Be at the meeting five to ten minutes before the scheduled time to make sure that you're the first person there. When they join in, you have to be the one to introduce them. You should brief the candidate about the interview structure and what to expect.

- **Selling the Job**

  To get the prospect to join the team, you have to sell them on why your job is better than all the rest. You want to do two things here.

  First of all, you want to tell them who you are and briefly introduce yourself. Why did you start your business, and why do you love what you do?

  Next, you want to give them a brief introduction about your company, laying out its values, positioning, vision, and mission.

- **The Discussion**

  During the discussion process, you want to maintain a frame. Just like with a sales call, the only things that should be coming out of your mouth are questions, anecdotal stories, and restatements. You need to lean heavily on the questions.

  Start with an open-ended question that allows the candidate to share their experience and their skills. A lot of interviewers say, "So, tell me a little bit about yourself." Try to change things up and appear unique. Does this question really match your brand and the energy you provide?

- **Role-Specific Questions**

  Ask questions that pertain specifically to the job's role to assess the candidate's suitability for it. Here, they should explain their relevant experiences to you.

- **Behavioral Questions**

  Use behavioral questions to understand how the candidate will react in a specific situation. For example, if you're hiring a sales rep, you might ask, "What would you do if the lead flow is slow?"

- **Competency-Based Questions**

  These questions are aimed at understanding the candidate's skills and abilities inside of the business. One question that can really identify an A-player is, "What are your weaknesses?" Many times, A-players won't just say the usual thing, like, "I work too fast" or "I'm too much of a perfectionist." That's what everyone says.

  An A-player will reply with a skill that isn't relevant to the job. For example, I might say that I'm really bad at Spanish when the job doesn't involve anything to do with Spanish. Then they'll show how they overcame the obstacle of not knowing it.

- **The Q&A**

  The next step is allowing the candidate to ask questions. This can give you an insight into the candidate's values and their interest in the role. Again, this should be used to check for cultural consonance, competence compatibility, and commitment congruence. This is an open session where you will answer anything they ask.

  Don't make them feel like they should be scared to ask you questions. It will backfire in the long run.

- **Conclusion**

  Wrap up the interview by summarizing some of the key points discussed in the interview. Next, you want to inform them of the steps to come. Let the candidate know what they should expect next in the hiring process. And last but not least, you want to thank the candidate. Show your appreciation for their time and their interest in the role. Even if you don't think they're a good fit, make sure to thank them because they might deliver some reciprocity in the form of a referral.

- **Post-Interview**

  Immediately after the interview, note down all your first impressions while they are still fresh. I use an internal form that gets filled out and adds them to the team CRM inside of the pipeline. You must evaluate quickly. The longer you wait, the more you will forget.

  The form should include speaking skills, the three pillars of the tri-harmony talent matrix, any additional notes you may have, and the meeting recording link. Keep the candidate updated on their status in the hiring process.

- **Making Decisions**

  It's very important to learn what factors to consider when deciding which candidate to hire and understand how to balance these factors against each other. My company is very energy-focused, so I hire off of heart and energy.

  If someone is fully committed, in my opinion, there's no way they can lose. This doesn't mean you should just hire the person you think has the most potential. Hire people who know what they are doing and who already have experience in the role, but also make sure the person is fun to be around.

116

Hiring Red Flags

Certain factors can immediately disqualify a prospect. Although they may vary, you should create a personalized list of specific disqualifications. Any elements that are "pet peeves" or hinder consistent collaboration should be considered disqualifying.

Here are a few examples that I use:

- If the prospective team member does not have their camera on—disqualify them.
- If they're not sharp with their words—disqualify them.
- If they're not dressed well—disqualify them.
- If they're not where their feet are or not present in the moment—disqualify them.
- If they are slow to respond to your test—disqualify them.
- If they don't submit a Loom video—disqualify them.
- If you are on the fence as to whether they will be a good fit—disqualify them.

These red flags are things that I have noticed make a bad team member. If you can disqualify them early on, they will save you a lot of headache and trouble in the hiring process and they will keep you from having to go through the firing process.

TL;DR: If something seems off, it probably is. Don't hire people who give off red flags.

Understanding A-Players

I rely on the ROLE (Results, Ownership, Learning, and Enthusiasm) framework to effectively identify and recruit top-tier talent. This framework enables me to streamline the hiring process, ensuring that I find individuals who possess the skills, expertise, and cultural fit necessary to thrive in their roles. With the ROLE framework, I can confidently build high-performing teams that drive success and achieve organizational goals.

Results

When evaluating a candidate, it is important to start by checking the results they have achieved in their previous roles. Consider what specific skills and qualities they can bring to your company, as well as the specific outcomes they can deliver. During the interview process, have them provide concrete examples, such as their sales numbers or notable accomplishments, and inquire about the strategies they employed to achieve these successes.

In addition to the end result, you want to find out how they accomplish these goals. This is different for every role, but finding their workflow speed and style is crucial. If a candidate took a large chunk of time to achieve a desired result and you require a more expedited approach, they may not be the best fit for the role.

Ownership

Ask questions that assess whether the candidate takes ownership of their projects and responsibilities. Good fits simply do not shy away from responsibility. They own up to their mistakes and let people know when there is a problem. One of the interview questions I ask is, "What is one time that you made a mistake, and how did you deal with it?" This question will give you an idea of how they think.

Learning

To identify A-players, you must assess their commitment to lifelong learning and development. This encompasses both professional growth and self-improvement. As part of my recent interview approach, I have started inquiring about the last book candidates have read or any new skills they have acquired.

If they are not eager to learn, they are not coachable. You don't want someone who is stagnant. You need someone who is coachable and looking to improve their life and income. It is very important to get an idea of how they operate in their life outside of business. The hard truth is that people want someone who is physically fit and has a good situation at home. If a team member comes into work with their problems, they drag down the efficiency of the team.

Enthusiasm

A-players have positive attitudes and unwavering enthusiasm towards their work. They are driven by the desire to achieve victory. Your job is to assess their passion for the role they're applying for and the company. It's best to steer clear of people with a negative outlook. Their attitude can dampen team dynamics and hinder overall success. If everyone is not rowing the boat at the same pace, it just goes in circles.

Attracting Talent

For reference, my best team members were applicants who went above and beyond to reach out to me. I'm not saying that you should just sit around and twiddle your thumbs and wait for someone to appear out of thin air, but I am saying that I think it's a huge indicator of a good prospect.

One of my video editors and thumbnail designers is a great example. When I posted the job interview, I got hundreds of applications, but he went above and beyond to send me a WhatsApp message and follow me on all my social media platforms. This made me instantly like him more and built rapport. Now he's one of the top-performing guys on the team.

Also, remember that winners typically are already winning inside of a company. Four out of five millionaires do not own their own business. This means that if you want to find really good people, you might have to headhunt other companies.

Don't steal from your friends; steal from your competitors. If the candidates can live a better life and make more money with you, it's all up to them.

The Magnet Framework

- **Mission**
  Top performers are motivated by more than just monetary rewards. They seek to be part of a greater purpose. That's why it is so important to clearly communicate your company's mission and vision statement and highlight how their role directly contributes to this mission. Their vision must fit in and align seamlessly with the overarching vision of the company.

- **Advancement**
  Provide potential A-players with a transparent roadmap for professional growth and career advancement within your organization. They should be able to envision a clear path towards higher-level roles, ensuring that their journey continues beyond any perceived limitations.

- **Growth**
  Highlight opportunities for personal growth, such as continuous learning, skill development, and challenging projects. Many A-players come to learn, not to earn. Yes, they still need money to live, and they know their worth, but often, they learn a lot from you as well.

- **Nurturing Culture**
  A-players flourish in a work culture that has positivity and support. You should highlight your company's culture, values, and

dedication, not just externally but also when it comes to the well-being of its employees.

One mistake I made early on was trying to treat everybody like family. Yes, your culture should foster a tight-knit community, but you also need to draw a line in the sand as to how far that should actually go.

- **Excitement**

Generate enthusiasm for the position, team, and projects they will be involved in. Energy is contagious. If people are sleepy and lazy, they are cancer. We want high-energy individuals who are ready to conquer.

- **Total Reward**

Beyond competitive salaries, A-players value comprehensive rewards packages. This can include benefits, flexible work options, recognition programs, and more. Yes, salaries are good, but the earning opportunity is the most important thing.

A-players are attracted to organizations where they can make a significant impact. Showcasing these opportunities is key. An A-player knows their worth and will have bigger needs for pay, but the cost is lower in the long run. When you lose a team member, it costs a lot more money than just paying a little bit more on the front end for an A-player.

Turning Your Team into an Army

- **Accountability**

Holding people accountable is your **obligation**.

If you don't, you're holding them back from their true potential.

You need to make sure there are no holes in the bucket and things are not slipping through the cracks.

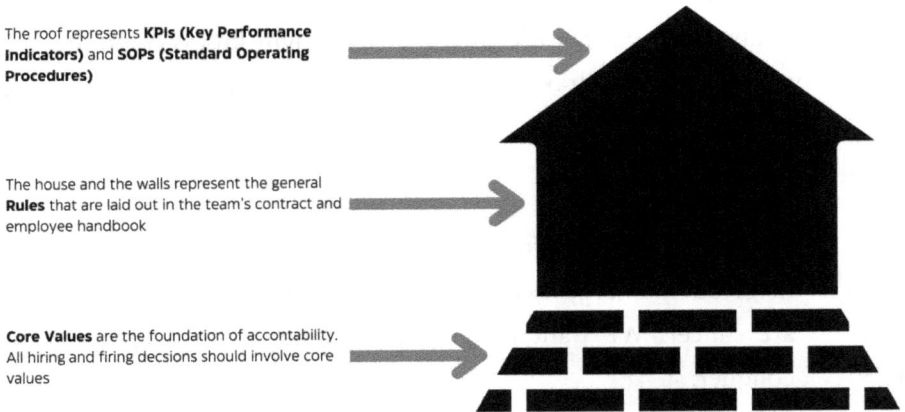

The roof represents **KPIs (Key Performance Indicators)** and **SOPs (Standard Operating Procedures)**

The house and the walls represent the general **Rules** that are laid out in the team's contract and employee handbook

Core Values are the foundation of accontability. All hiring and firing decsions should involve core values

Over time, I've developed my pyramid of accountability. At the bottom lies the foundation, the core values. Everything revolves around them. All decisions should be made with core values.

In the middle, we have the rules and the employee handbook. This is where you lay out each thing that employees should and should not do. Any policies you have should be listed here. It doesn't have to be long, and it shouldn't be just jargon.

And at the top are your standing operating procedures (SOPs) and key performance indicators (KPIs). The SOPs should lay out the exact way that people should do their jobs. The KPIs should lay out the result you expect them to get.

Communication Techniques

A slow response time is the biggest indicator that someone is not a good fit for my company. I mandate that my team members have their notifications on and reply within 15 minutes during their work hours. If they don't, they get one warning before they're fired.

Yes, this is strict, but it's called a standard.

Slack is the best application that I've found for this so far. Slack is essentially a chat platform that allows for quick and efficient communication. It also has features like file sharing, video calls, and integrations with other apps. If they have Slack on a desktop, they should make sure they have their notifications on at all times.

iMessage is another key to building an army because it fosters rapport and shows that you actually care about your people.

Elements of a Positive and Productive Company Culture

I'm going to focus on building culture for an online team rather than in person because I think this is the hardest thing for people to get.

If the leader does not lead by example, their team will not follow them to the right place.

A lot of people wildly underestimate the number of applications they should look over when hiring. For a VA role, I typically look at around three hundred to five hundred applications before deciding on one person.

And that's for a virtual assistant. Imagine if I were hiring for a bigger role.

What's just as important as hiring the right people is timely termination. If you don't fire quickly, you're going to spoil the company culture for everyone around you.

Finally, you need to make sure that you're sharing wins, personal, with clients, or with the business, in your Slack channels. This will help team members celebrate the wins of others and be celebrated when they win. It's an incentive.

Retaining Talent

RETAIN FRAMEWORK:

- **Recognition**
- **Engagement**
- **Training**

- **Advancement**
- **Incentives**
- **Nurturing Culture**

Recognition: Make sure you're regularly recognizing and rewarding employees for their hard work and achievements. This can be in the form of public recognition, awards, or even simple thank-you notes.

One of the biggest things I've learned from millionaire entrepreneurs and investors Alex and Leila Hormozi is to praise rather than punish. When you punish someone, you are reinforcing the decision not to do something whenever you're around, but as long as they don't get caught, it doesn't matter.

Engagement: It's very important to engage your team members in the decision-making process and seek their input on matters that affect their work. When you give them a sense of ownership, they feel valued and make better decisions on the company's behalf. Great intrapreneurs actually seek out roles where they feel like they have power.

Training: One of my core values is to continue learning. You should offer continuous learning opportunities to all of the people on your team. This should include personal and professional development.

Professional development helps employees get better in business, and personal development helps them get better in their personal lives so they can perform better when they're working. A lot of people overlook this part, but I think it is crucial. Such opportunities for development not only improve employees' skills but also show that you're invested in their professional and personal growth.

Advancement: You need to provide clear paths for career advancement within the organization. Employees are much more likely to stay if they see potential for moving up the ladder.

Incentives: Incentives go beyond competitive salaries. You need to offer financial and non-financial incentives. These can include bonuses, stock options, flexible work arrangements, wellness programs, etc. Get creative. This will help show how your army is special and different.

Nurturing Culture: You need to foster a positive and inclusive work culture that encourages teamwork, collaboration, and social interaction.

Leverage

So, why should you actually hire someone when you could do the job better yourself?

Well, the reason is for leverage.

You need to start replacing your lower-leverage tasks with a virtual assistant so you can focus on the higher-leverage tasks and make more money.

You owe it to your team.

You have to look at the opportunity cost of your time spent sitting around and working on the lower-leverage tasks.

Trust me; you can get a lot further ahead when someone else handles those tasks.

I like assistants in the Philippines the best because they speak almost perfect English. And for my East Coast U.S. folks, they're 12 hours off, which is perfect because they're always getting something done even when you're not.

When I'm looking for a virtual assistant, I'm looking for three things: do they have a certain job-specific skill set, are they well organized, and will they be able to take on tasks easily?

I need to see that they have ambition and drive to win. I'm also looking to see if they have authority, which I can find with a disk profile.

The biggest thing I'm looking for in anyone I hire is how developed their FITFO muscle is ("figure it the fuck out"). Problem solvers change the world.

Conclusion

I did not write this book to make money. In fact, I will most likely lose a good bit of money on it. I wrote it because my life's purpose is more than making money. While money makes your life better in every facet, if the world collapses, money doesn't matter.

My reason for writing this book is that I believe that entrepreneurs are the ones who change the world. Small businesses (whether brick and mortar or in person) rule our local economies, and without a thriving economy, we cannot have a thriving society.

Nothing changes until you change. Change starts with the individual. When you change, the people around you change. When the people around you change, society changes. And when society changes, the world changes.

So, I want to sincerely thank you for taking the time to read this book. You now have the tools and tactics to change the world. I hope that the information and insights shared in these pages have been valuable to you.

One of my core values is continued learning, so if you want to learn more specific tactical information and the exact strategies we use on a day-to-day basis, check out my inner circle. This group can provide you with a hundred times the information in this book. Information updates rapidly; books don't.

Are you ready to go to the next level?
Visit dozerdog.co/domination or scan
the QR code:

As an entrepreneur, your potential for success is unlimited. Dream big and take risks. And when you do achieve success, don't forget to give back and help others along their entrepreneurial journey. Go dominate life!

Thank you,

Zachary Bordeaux

THANK YOU FOR READING MY BOOK!

Thank you for reading my book! Here are a few free bonus resources.

Scan the QR Code Here:

I appreciate your interest in my book and value your feedback as it helps me improve future versions of this book. I would appreciate it if you could leave your invaluable review on Amazon.com with your feedback. Thank you!

www.ingramcontent.com/pod-product-compliance
Lightning Source LLC
Chambersburg PA
CBHW072156090426
42740CB00012B/2292

9 781963 793505